To: Courtney
Thx you for your —
— KC Rayple

Copyright

This is a work of fiction. Names, characters, businesses, places, events and incidents are either the products of the author's imagination or used in a fictitious manner. Any resemblance to actual persons, living or dead, or actual events is purely coincidental.

All rights reserved. This book or any portion thereof may not be reproduced or used in any manner whatsoever without the express written permission of the author except for the use of brief quotations in a book review. The following story contains mature themes, strong language, and sexual situations. It is intended for adult readers.

Copyright © 2015 by KC Royale

Dedication

George, Brian, Ricky and Samuel... My four brothers who are also my best friends in the whole world. It's a rare thing to find people who will LOVE you no matter what, but I am lucky enough to have four of them.

In Honor of

Those who aren't afraid to dream and fight each day to achieve the impossible. Those who are driven to send a message of happiness, fulfillment and positivity to the world through books

In Memory of

My beloved grandparents; Sylvester and Birdie May. Born into this world on May 4th and May 28th... I didn't have much time with either of you, but I cherish the love and time that I did have. May you both Rest in Peace.

"We are the music makers, and we are the dreamers of dreams…"

Poem; Ode
Recited by; Willy Wonka (Gene Wilder)
Written by; Arthur O'Shaughnessy

"What inspires one, can inspire another."

-KC ROYALE

Table of Contents

Chapter 1 1
Chapter 2 11
Chapter 3 21
Chapter 4 29
Chapter 5 40
Chapter 6 54
Chapter 7 70
Chapter 8 79
Chapter 9 88
Chapter 10 97
Chapter 11 112
Chapter 12 122
Chapter 13 130
Chapter 14 145
Chapter 15 156
Chapter 16 162
Chapter 17 176
Chapter 18 190

Chapter 19 202

Chapter 20 212

Epilogue 229

Author Note 244

The Scent of… MUSK 245

More Books by Author KC Royale 247

About the Author 249

Acknowledgements 250

Stalked For Love

Chapter 1

Have you ever felt as if you're being watched? I knew for a fact that a pair of eyes were on me... watching me, and perhaps following me. I used to feel a little paranoid, thinking that I actually had a stalker. It bothered me for a while, until I realized that I wasn't important enough to have anyone stalking me. The strange thing was that it no longer drove me insane, as much as it used too. But I still couldn't shake the eerie feelings that I would sometimes get, about my current situation.

It wasn't always easy for me being so far away from home, while attending college in another state. There were good times and there were definitely some bad times, when I really wished I was back home. But somehow I've managed to endure it all, by staying focused on my studies. One class at a time. A long yawn escaped me as I lay in my bed, just thinking about my life while also listening to the rain that was tapping my bedroom window, undoubtedly flooding the streets of our small town.

It was late, very late, and I should be sleeping right now. But there I lay with my eyes wide open, while nestled under my warm covers, thinking. I blew out an exaggerated breath, as my eyes roamed around my vast room. A room that now only held a few boxes, packed with my belongings. My room was located on the second floor of the house that a few of my friends and I were renting, while we attended college together.

We'd been living here for a little over three years now, but tonight was the last night that I would be living here. Because the day to move out had *finally* arrived, and I was very excited. Living in a house with six girls wasn't always the slumber party I thought it would be, when I agreed to move in. There were times when I appreciated the company, but then there were other times—when I really wished I was all alone, and living in my own place.

It wasn't always bad living here, but at times, it really was. Due to the fact that most of my roommates were actively dating, and having lots of sex. Which of course, resulted in an endless stream of noise and traffic, at all hours of the day and night. What can I say; the constant parties, flings and even the noise were no longer appealing to me.

I had evolved quite a bit, from when I was first finding my way, as a new college student. Back then, my anxiety from being all alone in a new state, had really bothered me. So when I saw the posting of rooms for rent, in an all-girl house, I immediately jumped on it.

But as the years passed, unfortunately the madness didn't end, it only grew. So much that it had unfortunately begun to affect *my* life, in more ways than one. It became difficult to read, study or even sleep most times. Which explains why I was still up at three-forty-three in the morning, while involuntarily listening to my roommate, Julie, getting her head thrashed into her wall, by her new boyfriend, Ian.

"Oh, Ian... thump thump, mmm don't stop... thump thump thump," Julie moaned loudly.

She lived right next door to me, right on the other side of the thin wall that separated our rooms. She'd sometimes spend nights out with her various boyfriends, but not tonight. Tonight she was home, with her newest boyfriend, who apparently has the stamina of a sexually charged stallion. So, for one more night, I fortunately got to hear why I was so excited to almost be free from this damned house.

I wasn't like this in the beginning, back then I was always up for some downtime fun with the gals. But now, all I wanted was some peace and quiet. So after finally securing myself a job and a new place to live, less than twenty miles away from campus. I only had one more night of this madness, and tomorrow would be a new day. A day when I was finally going to get what I wanted, a life of my very own.

***

Having done so all on my own, I would in no way allow anything or anyone to take away from this freeing moment of my impending independence. A new beginning was on the horizon for me, and I was determined not to let anything ruin that. Including the unsettling notion, that someone was *still* secretly watching me. It all started about a year ago, while I was walking home from a long day at the campus library.

I'd had a final to prepare for that week, so I was spending most of my evenings at the campus library, studying. Since my shared house was just entirely too noisy. While walking home that night, it was eerily quiet and the streets were practically empty.

I found myself picking up my pace as I strode home, before my mild anxiety got the best of me. I thought I'd seen someone out the corner of my eye a few times. But it was dark and I was tired, so I brushed it off. Until I had *actually* seen someone at the next corner with my own two eyes, looking straight at me.

It was definitely a man, I could tell by his silhouette. He wasn't walking or pacing, he just stood still... a little too still. But I'd kept walking, while cautiously glancing behind me, only to see that there was no-one around. When I'd turned back towards him, he was still there, staring. We were surprisingly alone, which was very unusual, especially on a street near a college. But, we were in fact, alone. Suddenly, a wave of panic washed over me and I immediately stopped walking.

I began to check my surroundings again and I still didn't see anyone around. It was already dark outside, and the streets weren't as populated as they normally were in the day. The only people in that short block at that very moment, were the two of us. I had a gut feeling that this was not good. I quickly calculated that there were less than thirty steps between us, from where I was now standing.

As my mind roamed, he still didn't move an inch. I narrowed my eyes at him, trying to see if I could recognize him, but I just couldn't see him clearly. It was hard to see anything outside of his masculine frame, not to mention that he'd worn all black and stood a short distance away. I was near the beginning of the short block, and he was near the end of that same block. I glanced around once more, and from what I could see, there were only two people walking, and they both happened to be on the *other* side of the street.

A few cars were passing by and I glanced back at the man, and he was still there, staring at me. I took a deep breath and as I exhaled, I tried to think of what to do. I didn't want to seem panicky and just start running, as if he had a machete in his hand, looking to chop me into pieces. But the longer I stood there contemplating his motives and my impending actions, the more I found myself almost at full panic attack mode. I then took a few lingering steps, in the direction of the mysterious stranger, hoping he would just turn around and walk away, but he didn't.

My steps faltered the closer I got to him, as my nerves began taking over my mind and my ability to walk. Ironically, in a matter of about two minutes, I'd only managed to take a few steps forward. Just then, a small crowd of students emerged out of a door, just near the strange man. They walked around him, on either side as if he wasn't even standing there. The man just stood there, not even flinching as he continued to just stare at me.

With no visible streetlights where he stood, all I could make out additionally, was his baseball cap that appeared to be either black or blue, with some kind of white lettering that glimmered on occasion. As I took another lingering step forward, someone had bumped into me while rushing out of the nearby shop, I was unknowingly standing in front of.

"Oh, I'm so sorry," she murmured, to me. "Oh crap, I knocked your bag down. I'm sorry, my ride is waiting for me and I was stuck waiting while they brewed fresh coffee." she said, bending down to help me pick up my book bag.

I then glanced over her shoulder, flinching my eyes at the store that was surprisingly still open. I hadn't noticed at all, that this store was still open, this late at night. Most of the stores on the campus strip closed early, but I was never one to stay out lingering around much, so I had no clue that some actually stayed opened this late. I then turned to see the girl standing while holding my bag out towards me.

She kept apologizing and calling herself clumsy, as I smiled at her. But I was in fact grateful for her clumsiness, and her perfect timing. *If she only knew how perfect her timing really was.* I quickly turned back to see the man at the corner... but he was no longer standing there. As I frantically glanced around, there was no sign of him anywhere. It was like he'd just vanished without a trace. My eyes continued to scour the street, but to no avail. *He was gone.*

"Oh, well, it happens. Thank you, and have a good night," I muttered, as she smiled at me. She then continued on her way, running towards the car that was waiting for her, on the other side of the street. I swung my bag over my shoulder and waited for a moment to gather my thoughts.

I then dug inside my bag and grabbed my mace and clutched it in my hand, before I placed my other hand inside my hoodie pocket. I then pulled my hood over my head, and started to walk the rest of the way home. That night was very different from the other nights I'd walked home alone from the campus library. Because that night, the entire walk home felt very strange. I just couldn't shake the feeling that with each step I took… I was being followed.

Ever since that night, I have kept looking over my shoulder, wondering if I was still being watched. There were days when I wouldn't feel anything out of the ordinary, and things would be great. Then there were days when I was on edge, and felt that unsettling twist in my stomach. It was the same gut reaction that I'd felt that very night, when I saw *him*, just standing there, watching me.

As the months passed, I kept pondering who this guy really was, and why out of all people would he want to watch me. I found myself wondering if he was still around the area, lurking in the bushes while observing me. Somehow, I knew he was still out there. I just couldn't shake the feeling, and I would soon discover that my gut feeling, was indeed right.

Chapter 2

I covered my mouth to shelter the yawn that was coming up from deep inside, as my professor gave his lecture today. I was so tired, and I had so many things to do after class. Just the thought of what those things entailed, made me even more tired. Not to mention that I only managed to get two hours of sleep last night. Thanks to my roommate, Julie, and her boy toy, Ian. I sat there quietly at my desk but the truth was, I was already bored with this lecture.

This lecture was one of the last ones I'd ever have to hear, so I listened, but I was also distracted at the same time. It was Friday, and my entire weekend was fully booked, which has never really happened before. So while in class, I found myself mentally writing a to-do list, while I scribbled illegibly on my notepad. The school year was finally coming to an end. Graduation was days away, and I couldn't be happier.

One week from now; I would be a college graduate, settled in my new place, and starting a new job soon after. *Hmm, not too shabby.* I thought, as I smirked to myself. "Something funny, Miss Moore?"

A firm voice had snapped me out of my mental deliberations, as I turned and made eye contact with *him*, my Professor. Once I saw the forbidden look on his face, a shiver ran through me, making me squirm. As if on cue, just like a synchronized swimming team, the entire lecture hall turned to stare at me. Professor Brennan had never complained when I would stare off into space while he lectured before, but I guess he wanted my undivided attention today.

But with only a few classes left, why would he choose right now to put me on the spot, in front of everyone? They all just stared at me, and I was flushed in embarrassment and very surprised at Professor Brennan's annoyance, but not for the reasons you may think. Professor Brennan knew that I wasn't like some of the other students, the ones who were barely progressing in his class. Oh no, I actually *wanted* to excel in my studies, and always took every available job, and extra credit assignment he'd offered.

In doing so, it helped me to advance in many ways throughout my academic career. So he knew I would always apply myself to his expert-tutelage, and I didn't allow myself to become distracted. I was there to learn, and that's what I did. Which is why I was so surprised by the tone he was using with me. He'd never used this tone with me before, or with anyone in my class. He always used a somewhat leveled tone when he spoke, an inviting tone if you will, that was *always* free from wrath.

I always assumed that, Professor Brennan was a person who probably didn't get angry too often. He just exudes that type of demeanor, a very calm and controlled kind of persona. Therefore, the tone he was using with me at the moment, was definitely unheard before, literally. As I found myself just staring back at him, utterly speechless.

I noticed that his stare had now turned into a glare, as he impatiently waited for me to speak. But I was at a loss for words, I couldn't speak to save my life. *What was wrong with me?* "My office, after class." he stated, as I swallowed rather loudly.

"Yes, professor," I muttered, and again the whole lecture hall turned back around, and began to ignore me, as they normally did. I self-consciously glanced around and saw that the attention was now off of me, and I exhaled. I didn't like attention, and I especially didn't like bad attention. It was rare moments like this, when I was very glad that college was almost over.

We had less than twenty minutes left in this lecture, and I had managed to get in trouble for the first time, in all my three years in his classes. I didn't like it. I had never been told to see one of my professors after class, especially the one who I actually respected the most. But I guess there was a first time for everything, even if it happens when you only have four more days of college left.

I couldn't believe that I actually disrupted his lecture and got somewhat reprimanded in front of everybody. *Great going, Jess.* I really didn't like that I was told to see him after class, at the very end of my time at college. I hoped that the worst I would get from him was a verbal warning, if that. I took a deep breath as I stared at him as he spoke so intelligently, and then I glanced down towards the front two rows, that was filled with those google-eyed women.

The woman who wanted him so badly, they should have written *please fuck me* on their foreheads. Yes, Professor Brennan was impressive, so impressive that he has an actual fan club. Can you BELIEVE IT? *A freaking fan club.* Out of all the professors here at Morgan State University, he was the most admired, which had generated an intense group of female fans. I never joined, but I understood why it existed. The man was gorgeous, stylish and very smart. He was the complete package.

When I use the word gorgeous, I don't mean simply gorgeous, I meant breathtakingly gorgeous. He was tall, with black short hair, soft hazel eyes and a light five o'clock shadow that fit him perfectly. I could tell from how well he dressed for class each day, that his body was long and properly proportioned, it wasn't hard at all to size him up. Besides, not just anyone would be deemed *impressive* in my book.

I would sometimes gaze at him while thinking how remarkable he must be in bed, but then I'd rid myself of those thoughts when I remembered that he was my professor. But seeing him daily in his tailored suits was always a beautiful sight in itself, especially the way his suit pants hung low on his hips.

Oh, and his voice was deep and worldly, like a warm salty breeze off the coast. He always spoke in a smooth and very educated way, making all the ladies giggle in the front two rows. Which is why I always sat in the back with the guys, so I didn't have to hear his fan club distracting me too much.

I didn't want to be too distracted while in class, so I sat where I could concentrate more aptly. Since I really didn't take too much interest in the boys at college, I had nothing to worry about while sitting in the back with the guys. Because I, Jessica Moore, was a good enough distraction to myself, so I really didn't need any help in that area, whatsoever.

It was more than just that; I wanted to be different and I wanted to succeed in life. I just didn't want to end up telling the same story that everyone else would tell. *"When I was in college I partied, got drunk, had lots of sex, and barely passed my classes. The End.*" NO!! That was not going to be my story at all, and I was very happy and proud to say, that it wasn't.

I worked my ass off to do the best I could for these past four years, and had succeeded in my goals. Now I was days away from graduation, with a 3.8 GPA. I had already secured a job, which to any normal college student was pretty freaking amazing. I was very proud of myself, and how far I'd come. So I never allowed myself to read too much into the gorgeous Professor Brennan, for two important reasons. I was determined to stay focused at all times and he was simply out of my league.

I exhaled and glanced down the row I was in and saw all the guys staring ahead, while a few sheepishly glanced over at me smiling. I gave back a tight smile in return, before turning back towards Professor Brennan, who was now *staring* at me, again. *Oh crap*! I knew I was definitely getting a warning now, as I groaned inwardly.

I would have to talk to him and make him understand, that I am sorry for being so, distracted today. I smiled and sat up straighter as he continued on with his lecture. I really didn't want anything on my record, not one blemish. So I decided to save my roaming thoughts for later, and pay attention for the remainder of the class. I then glanced at my watch, and saw that we had only ten minutes left, and as I exhaled…

"Class dismissed. Miss Moore, my office, now." he stated, and packed his bag and left the lecture hall. I nodded my head and quickly packed my bag, feeling the anxiety seeping into my veins. Once from behind my desk, I started walking towards the staircase, joining the long line of students trying to get to the bottom. Once I neared the bottom, I could hear the members of his fan club giggling and talking rather loudly and very inappropriately.

"I wish he'd call *me* into his office after class, he'd never forget it." A girl named Melissa giggled as she swung her blond hair over her shoulders.

"That man will haunt my dreams even after graduation, and many years to come." A girl named Nicole stated, as she slowly licked her lips, and closing her eyes. They all began giggling again, until another girl spoke.

"As you all know, I have first dibs on *that sexy ass man*. Before I leave this school and by my calculations, I have less than a week... to taste him, and I will." Said the girl who was known as the *president* of his fan club, no doubt his number one fan. She made her crass statement with such an arrogance and determination, that I actually narrowed my eyes at her.

Her name was, Joy White, she was beautiful, popular and very rich. She had women envying her, and she always had guys begging her for a date. So when and how she set her sights on our Professor, was a mystery to me, but that didn't stop her. Because rumor has it that a year ago is when she started his fan club, and the rest is history.

Professor Brennan was a man who probably had to literally fight the ladies off with a stick. *What a hard life that must be for him?* Nonetheless, all of them were in total denial to want this man so badly. He was our professor for goodness sake, and it was quite obvious that he was unattainable. However handsome he was, it still didn't change the fact that he was a part of the faculty. There were very strict policies in place about fraternizing and so forth, to put it simply, it was strictly forbidden. But I could tell that quite a few of his admirers didn't care too much about that, which was just insane to me. *Why risk your academic career over anyone?*

I was so glad those girls were graduating, so they could end this childless obsession over our teacher. I just looked at them as they continued to giggle and chat openly about their infatuation with him, they were really pathetic. I quickly headed out the door, because I had other things on my mind, like, my move. I only had a few more boxes to pack before driving up to my new place, for good. So I hoped I wasn't in too much trouble with Professor Brennan, because I needed to be on my way, as soon as possible.

Chapter 3

To have an extreme interest in someone can sometimes become unhealthy, and can quickly become a fixation. A natural interest can easily become compulsive, and one could quickly lose control over their infatuation. When someone is obsessed, they've lost control of their feelings about the object of that obsession. Obsession; if there was a doubt what the word meant, there was none now. Professor Brennan is a man who is learning just how deep an obsession can overrun his actions as well as his emotions.

This was a man who had lost control over his feelings about her a very long time ago, triggering an intense infatuation that was beginning to influence his everyday life. There were times when he couldn't even recognize himself, because he was so far gone. He just couldn't control himself at times. Just the thought of her, has his heart pounding in his chest, and his body quivering in adulterated lust. He was a man whose interest in a woman had truly become unhealthy and compulsive.

It's been three years since he first laid eyes on her, and his world was immediately turned on its head. It was more than just her smooth skin, long blond hair and shimmering blue eyes that had him so distracted. It was her character, her drive, her determination and guile, to be whom *she* wanted to be in this world. She was strong and capable of becoming so many things in her life, and he wanted her to be *his*.

This woman had truly done the impossible, and reopened his heart in ways that are refreshingly new, and irreversible. With his need to be closer to her, completely consuming his entire being, things were really getting to him. He was beginning to allow his irrational emotions, to overrule his rational thinking. He knew that lately, his actions were dangerous, erratic and the most extreme.

His fixation on this one woman had him doing things, that he'd never thought himself capable of doing. Because his fixation on this one woman had consumed him whole. His fixation on this woman could put him and his career in jeopardy. But there was no way he was giving her up, ever. He had no clue how to even start the process, or when the time would finally come for him to proceed. But it didn't stop the path of his dreams for the two of them. He could already see them growing old together. He could see them being happy, and deeply in love.

As graduation nears, he knows that his time is running out and he needs to act fast. But he worries; this fixation of his on this one woman had a downside that he's had to accept. Which was him finding a discrete way to be closer to her, which was all that he's ever wanted, but it seemed impossible to have. But he's found a way, but at what cost? This secret obsession and need of his to be closer to her ... had become her worst nightmare.

***

Today was Friday, a very important Friday because school would be over in a few days. So by next Friday, she would no longer be his student. He didn't know if that made him extremely happy or extremely anxious as he looked at her, sitting in her normal seat inside the lecture hall. Every few minutes his gaze moved to her, as if he had no control over his own actions at this point.

He found himself subtly watching her as she continued to look out a small window, which was something she did quite often, when she was thinking about something. He could tell that she obviously had something on her mind, and it wasn't him.

In a lecture hall crowded with sixty students, he could barely concentrate. Jessica Moore was always on his mind, in ways that most would deem wrong, or disreputable. But he didn't have time to care about that anymore, because time was running out. She would be graduating soon and he didn't know what he was going to do. She was the one he wanted, the one he needed, but she was still his student… for four more days.

With each day that passed, it was getting harder for him. The pressure was mounting; the sleepless nights were increasing; all because of one insufferable dilemma. He still hadn't figured out how to go about moving his relationship with Jessica Moore forward, and out of uncharted territory.

What had started as just a veiled attraction had turned into a very powerful yearning. What he thought about doing with her was forbidden, and unethical for one in his position. Nothing could take away from the fact that she was a student, who for three years, had taken his classes. But to him, she was so much more than a student. Now, she was an obsession, *his* obsession.

She was the one who haunted his dreams. She was the one he desperately wanted, the one he desperately craved. It was so much more than mere interest, meager attraction, or even heated desire. He wanted her so badly, that he actually felt inadequate to surrender. He no longer knew how to stop the train of his thoughts of one day being with her. Or worse, the fear in his heart of never having her as his own. There was nothing more frustrating than wanting someone that you couldn't have.

He found out very quickly, that it took a high level of discipline, to keep his feelings for her under wraps, and he'd succeeded. But over time, his longing had progressed into something else entirely. Something forbidden… something untamed… something that had completely overwhelmed him.

As he continued with his lecture, he kept wondering what was on her mind, as his brow furrowed periodically. Even as the minutes passed, he could see that her mind was obviously *not* on his lecture, and that began to irritate him. He then noticed a soft smile began spreading across her lips, while she stared out the small window, obviously still deep in thought. Immediately he became jealous, because he knew he wasn't the reason for her smile.

He couldn't take it anymore. Her obvious distraction today had pushed him over the edge and he wanted her attention, and he knew just how to bring her thoughts back to him—or at least back to the room.

"Something amusing, Miss Moore?" He watched as her gaze moved towards his, and locked. He could see the light blush starting to cover her cheeks, as she flushed in embarrassment. Her fingers tightened on the pen she absently held, her grasp so tight that her knuckles began to turn white. He could actually feel the coiled tension in her body steady tightening, as she sat there silently gazing at him.

His eyes never left hers as he gazed at her reactions, silently. While his mind raced, vividly imagining what it would feel like to cause those exact reactions from her; but in a very *different* way. He then realized just how much things had progressed with him, far more than he'd ever thought possible. She was special to him, one of a kind special—and she had no idea. He found himself watching her as she looked at him speechless, still in shock obviously that he'd caught her being distracted.

"My office, after class," he snapped.

"Yes, professor," she muttered.

He continued on with his lecture, but he kept wondering what exactly was on her mind, but it no longer mattered to him now. It all played in his favor. Because of her being distracted, he found a way to use that to his advantage. In less than twenty minutes, he would be seeing her alone after class, and that was something he was already looking forward to.

He knew it was time to open the door for communication for them, and not as teacher and student. Because time was not on his side, and he didn't know how he was going to see her once graduation was over. She had so much happening for her already; he knew that she was moving and starting a new job soon. So how would he begin his decent into her life? That question alone has haunted him every day, up until a few months ago. When he'd finally thought of a plan, one that he would ensure, paid off.

Chapter 4

I made my way to Professor Brennan's office, walking down the crowded hall, with my bag slung over my shoulder and a smile on my face. I took in the scenery, realizing that these would be some of the last memories I would have of college. In the next week I would have moved, graduated, while also preparing to start work soon. I turned the corner, and began approaching the professors' office.

I knew where his office was, but I'd never been invited inside, until now. Which didn't make me feel any better about the conditions of *why* I had been invited inside, at this very moment. As I read his name card I swallowed and knocked three times, and waited. I turned around behind me to see some of my peers, who were happily roaming the halls, paying me no attention. They were all just so excited to finally be finishing school, so they could go on about their lives now, including me.

Most of the kids I knew were *told* they were going to college, and there was never a choice for them. But for me, I actually wanted to go, and begged my parents to help me get there. They paid for my tutoring throughout high school, because I was very bad at math, once upon a time. As well as my SAT prep, and here I am. Jessica Moore, an only child who was about to graduate college with honors, and be on my way in life.

I took a deep breath of gratification, and when I turned around to knock again, I was surprised to see that the door was now opened. There he was, looking at me with an unreadable expression on his face. *Professor Brennan.* He was just standing there, holding his door open for me as I blanched, clearly startled. *How long was I daydreaming?*

"Um, he-hello Professor Brennan," I muttered, feeling bashful all of a sudden.

"Miss Moore, how nice to see that you are *still* very much distracted," he murmured, as he waved for me enter.

I gave him a tight smile as I walked inside, and he closed the door after me. I stood there looking around this office, at his furniture and decor. I took a moment to take it all in, as I stood in the middle of the massive office, looking at the paintings that hung on the walls. There were a few gorgeous Monet paintings, I knew they were Monet's because he was my favorite painter. There were also a few hanging quotes by Hemmingway, that were carved in some type of stone.

The décor was typical; shiny cherry oak bookshelves lined most of the walls. There was a small couch and table near the window, and a desk and chairs. *Typical.* But as my eyes roamed, they landed back on that Monet painting, and I sighed.

"Beautiful," I muttered to myself, as I found myself lost in translation, lost in the pure beauty of this gorgeous painting.

"I'd like to think so," he murmured, breaking me out of my admiration. I cleared my throat and looked over to see that he was standing directly beside me. He was so close that his shoulder was almost touching mine. I then glanced down at his shoulder before looking back up at his face. I quickly noticed that his facial features were soft and inviting, as usual, but his eyes were burning into mine... his stare was almost magnetic.

I could tell that Professor Brennan is a passionate man, because he has such an odd intensity about him. It wasn't too intense to be deemed scary, but intense enough to be controlled. A man such as himself, probably was disciplined and had very strict parents in his upbringing. He just seemed as if he was very good at holding his emotions at bay, but it also looked as if his intensity could be triggered. I inhaled and swallowed hard at the discerning concentration of his gaze.

I wondered if he was alright, or if something happened with his family that had him so *off* today. He did seem as if he was on edge, when he's normally cool as a cucumber. I wanted to ask him, but it would be over-stepping my bounds. Surprisingly, my eyes were still locked on his, and I felt a shift. Suddenly, I didn't feel like I was in the principal's office any more, I sort of felt like I was in the office of a predator.

"Everything you see in this office is priceless to me," he muttered, while continuing to gaze at me. I had never heard his voice so soft before, it sounded so intimate, so, alluring.

"What's priceless?" I muttered, it took me a few minutes to figure out what he was talking about, as we continued to gaze at each other. *Oh the paintings!* Wow, someone could get lost in those eyes of his.

"Umm, shall I sit?" I asked, to break the unnerving eye contact between us.

"Yes, please have a seat," he gestured to a chair. I walked over and sat in one of the two chairs that were in front of his desk, as he followed me. To my surprise he didn't go and sit behind his desk chair, he came and sat beside me, in the other chair in front of his desk, the second chair.

"Miss Moore, I saw that you were very distracted during my lecture today. Would you mind explaining to me what was going on?" he asked as I stared straight ahead at his *empty* leather chair. I didn't know why I felt nervous all of a sudden, but I was.

"Professor, I'm so very sorry that I was distracted. I just…"

"Excuse me, but please look at me when you're speaking to me, Miss Moore," he murmured. I turned towards him, looking directly into his eyes, and he then nodded for me to continue.

"It's just that...I have some big changes happening this weekend, and I guess I'm a little nervous," I explained.

"What kind of changes?" he asked. I didn't know why I felt so nervous around him all of a sudden, especially when the school term was just about over. Maybe it was the fact that we never got personal in our conversations. Whenever we would talk, it was always about my schooling. Each and every single lecture, tutoring session, or even his extra credit seminars. Work, Work, Work... well, until now.

"I am moving this weekend, Professor. Well, actually I am almost finished moving my things, and I will be moving in tonight."

"Oh, well that's good, no need to be nervous. You're in transition, and there isn't anything wrong with that," he stated, confidently.

"I guess not, but..." I hesitated.

"But?" He urged.

"My life is going to be so different after next week. Having moved, graduated, and starting a new job, all in the same breath." I exhaled a shaky breath.

"Consider yourself lucky, Jess. It took me almost half a year after college, to have all that lined up before I started graduate school. I remember when I was in transition, I felt overwhelmed and somewhat terrified with everything I had on my plate. Trust me, just because you may start out feeling overwhelmed, doesn't mean you will stay that way. You've worked very hard for this and you're on your way. You've got this in the bag," he nodded, confidently as he smiled at me. *Did he just call me Jess?*

"Umm, I didn't know all that." I smiled back at him blinking a few times, feeling a wave of fresh air as he spoke about his time in college.

"You really don't know much about me outside of academia. When we're together, you're either studying or I'm tutoring you," he murmured.

"I didn't know that I could or, would ever, really get the chance to know you, outside of academia, Professor."

"Well, maybe you will now. You won't be my student in four more days, and then... all bets are most definitely *off*," he replied darkly. *All bets are what?* I felt my cheeks turning red as the blush covered my face, and I turned away from his gaze to get some distance. I knew in my gut that he was definitely flirting, yet not flirting at the same time. *Now this was a surprise. What was going on here?*

"Um, Professor Brennan, are you... flirting with me?" I asked.

"Now, Miss Moore, if I were flirting with you... I'm certain that you wouldn't have to ask me for confirmation on the matter, because you'd already know... for a fact," he stated.

"Um, okay," I replied, and tried to calm my nerves as I glanced back at him, to see him staring into my eyes again. I was sure he could see the uneasy look on my face, because hell, even I could feel it. I then swallowed rather loudly, as I tried to distract myself, by focusing on breathing in and out. Which at the moment seemed very difficult to do.

"Miss Moore, you are my student... for now, and I am your professor. Case closed.

Now, tell me about this job you've secured," he murmured.

I turned back towards him, to see that he'd crossed his leg. His ankle was resting on his knee, while both his hands were splayed on his thighs, almost as if he was willing himself to keep them there. I blinked up at him, and wondered why he was so inquisitive about my personal life all of a sudden.

He had never even so much as hinted at *anything* outside of academia, and now I wasn't sure if I could repeat that same statement in truth. I knew in my gut that I had nothing to worry about with Professor Brennan, because he wasn't a predator. He was always professional and respectful, and he would help me in any way that he could, and he has.

Besides, he has a fan club already, of some of the most willing and most beautiful girls in the entire university, pining after him. So there was no way that he was actually flirting with me. This was a man who had options, and I was sure I wasn't one of them. Furthermore, I knew that the director of my new internship would be calling him for my academic reference, if they hadn't already.

So I needed to not piss Professor Brennan off, to ensure that my reference would be a good one. So in-spite of my reservations to talk about my personal life, I found myself spilling my guts to him. To my surprise, he sat and listened attentively as I talked, and I could tell he was very interested in what I was saying. He'd kept a somewhat blank face, but he engaged me when needed, and I appreciated that. But at times, he seemed very distracted himself. *Odd!*

It was uncommon for me to talk about myself, not just to him, but to anyone. But then the strangest thing happened once I'd stopped talking to take a few breaths. He had actually started to talk to me, to me. I sat there stoned faced while he told me more about his time in college, and his first teaching job out of grad school. He also told me that he was thinking of leaving the university, and I was completely flabbergasted.

The man didn't look a day over thirty, and had an amazing job that he obviously loved. So how could he just up and leave this place? But if that was what he wanted to do, I wish him luck.

He must really trust me to just tell *me* something like that, and although I thought he would elaborate on that revelation, he didn't. To a great extent, I knew he was just trying to make me feel comfortable, so he may have been lying about leaving the university. Who knows? But what I did know was that today would no longer just be the day I got reprimanded in class for the first time. Oh no, today was so much more than that now.

Today would mark the day when I was allowed to see a different side of Professor Brennan, and even though the whole experience was a little jarring, it was also kind of sweet. But hearing him talk about his personal life, was not as easy as I thought it would be. I was very nervous as we were talking, I was actually trembling. Professor Brennan was just too much to take right now.

Being alone with him in his office like this was overpowering me, but I liked it. I liked that we were talking openly with each other for the first time ever. It was refreshing. I wasn't sure if knowing anything about him outside of the classroom would be a good thing at all. But, since I didn't have any plans to return to the college after graduation, I knew we wouldn't see one another again after next week. Or so I thought.

Chapter 5

I had a long drive ahead of me and after I'd packed up the last of my boxes, I'd hit the road. I was so happy to finally be out of that house, so it was a very happy day for me. I was now on the road leaving town, and it felt damned good. I was leaving all the madness, all the noise and all of my stalker memories behind me. I merged onto the parkway and was now passing a sign for Peter's Bar and Grill. The site of that sign alone had my stomach in knots and my pulse racing. Because now, I couldn't stop thinking about what almost happened to me, after leaving Peter's Bar and Grill, just a few weeks ago.

***

A few weeks ago... I was leaving a bar near campus, called Peter's. I was with a group of friends, and we all had more than a few beers that night. We were walking home from the bar, and we weren't even a full two blocks away when I suddenly felt my senses scattering. I started to look around, feeling like something was out of place.

The hairs on the back of my neck stood, as my breathing sped up. I didn't know if I was over reacting or just drunk, but what I felt was very disturbing, and sent me into a serious state of paranoia. Due to the fact that I could *feel* a pair of eyes on me.

"Hey, what are you looking at?" Sherry asked, while walking to stand beside me. Sherry was one of my roommates and she and I got along the most, out of all the girls the house. She was who I considered to be my best friend. She must had realized that I had stopped walking beside her, and turned to see that I was looking around for something... or better yet someone.

I hadn't seen *him* again since that first time on the street, which was eleven months ago. He hasn't made any appearances whatsoever since then, but that didn't make me feel very good. Because I still had a feeling he was still out there, watching me. I could feel it in my bones, just like I could tonight. Even though my brain was fogged from beer, I could still tell that something was off... I could just, feel it.

"Oh, nothing… I just thought I saw someone," I muttered, but the anxiety had already begun to overcome me.

"Okay, you have had a few too many beers young lady, as my father would say." Sherry waved her finger at me, teasing me as her words slurred. We both began to laugh while hugging each other; she was very funny at times. But she was right, I did have a few too many beers, and I'm not a big drinker.

A glass or two of good wine was more my speed, not beer. But there were a few times when I decided to *not* be the outcast of the group. You know the one everyone tries to pressure to chug beer, and not sip wine. To take shots, and not sip wine. To have cocktails, and not sip wine. Yeah, that was the normal prognosis, when I would go out to the bar with friends. Then somehow the entire night would become about; how to get Jess drunk tonight, and *not* off of wine. But tonight, I decided to beat them to the punch. I had planned to forgo my wine, and just drink with them to enjoy one of our last nights out together.

"Yeah, maybe I've had a few too many," I

giggled, while looking behind me and over across the street, still feeling an uneasy twisting in my stomach.

No one ever believed me, when I mentioned the guy I'd seen almost a year ago. They all just said that whoever I saw that night, was just a figment of my imagination. But I knew he was real, and I knew what I saw and that's all that mattered.

The four of us continued to walk home, passing a few more blocks, and then I felt it again. The hairs on the back of my neck stood, my breathing changed, and I knew that *his* eyes were watching me. I just couldn't shake the feeling, so I stopped walking, and began to glance around again. *Where are you, you bastard?*

They always say; be careful what you ask for. A moment later, I discovered exactly what they meant. Because as I turned back around towards my friends, I saw someone out the corner of my eye. My head immediately snapped back, and into the face of *him*. It was him… standing right there.

He was across the street in all black again,

with a dark baseball cap on, just staring back at me. I found myself gasping as I tried to call out to my friends, to ensure that someone saw him this time, other than me.

But my voice was taken from me, and I was frozen solid. Sadly, my friends were too drunk to notice anything at the moment. They had continued to walk while joking around and laughing, not even noticing that I was no longer walking beside them.

There were quite a few people out tonight on the streets, but somehow, all I could see was him. I just stared back at him, while taking a few things into account this time. He was tall and slim, but not particularly thin, and he was dressed in black clothing. He wore a cap with lettering that looked like it was a "NY" written in white. I didn't even take a moment to think before I dashed out into the traffic, trying to make my way across the street.

With each step I took, the more I found myself wanting to see his face. This man would *not* continue to haunt me, especially when he made such rare appearances. I have only seen him twice in eleven months, but in my gut I knew that meant nothing at all. I knew he was still around, watching me all the other times when I couldn't see him, which was just *insane* to me.

I was a girl who was only here to further her education, and I wasn't rich or popular. I was nobody important, so I didn't understand why he was doing this. It was settled, I wanted to know who he was. My mind was made up. *I was going to see who this man was, tonight!* The danger, and insanity of my actions, didn't even register to me. I was already numb because of my time at the bar earlier that night, and also from the insanity of this situation. *Who was this man?*

Maybe he was just a student in my university, who did this for fun to scare women. Or he could be the maniac who was just released from prison, that I've been imagining him to be. Either way, I was not going to take this lying down, anymore. The identity of this man has consumed me long enough. I was going to see who he was, and ask him a few questions of my own.

Why was he following me? What did he want

from me? Why won't he stop this? I was going to demand answers, right then and right there. I kept my eyes on him, hardly blinking as I walked right into the street. I was *not* going to lose him this time, or be distracted by something as silly as blinking. But the loud sound of a horn, and the screeching of tires, had managed to *actually* distract me, breaking through my beer induced brain freeze.

My head snapped around and I gasped... a huge truck was heading straight for me. The screaming tires, I realized, were from a huge truck swerving. The truck driver was desperately trying to stop his impending impact. It all was happening so fast. Horns blowing, tires screeching, while people were yelling incoherently. Then, there I was, frozen in place, while in the middle of the street.

The shock of it all had me frozen solid, and disabled my motor functions. The only movement I could manage was my throat and my eyes, as I swallowed a mouthful of saliva, while my eyes widened so wide they actually began watering.

The view in front of me was horrific, it was

surreal. There were two massive headlights that were rapidly approaching me, head on. I couldn't move, I couldn't' think, I couldn't even breathe. I was completely paralyzed, as a pair of strong arms grabbed me, and yanked me sideways. I was yanked so hard, that both of us fell onto the pavement with a very loud thud, as my face landed on a hard chest.

Someone broke my fall, and pulled me from an almost certain death. *Who? What? How?* I could hear a heart beating very fast, and I wasn't sure if it was mine, or maybe the one who just rescued me? I just tried to focus on breathing in and out. I took in deep breaths of air, as a soft and masculine scent began to surround me. While the arms that held me wrapped around me tighter, his nose buried in my hair as he inhaled deeply.

He held me so tightly that I couldn't move an inch, and I wasn't sure I wanted to, a part of me loved being held so intimately. Thank God I was still alive, but I felt woozy and my vision was blurry, very blurry. My head felt like it weighed a ton, and my limbs were too heavy to move. It took all of my strength to lift my head, and look into the face of the one who'd saved my life. But I couldn't see anything but skin and a parted mouth, since my vision was so blurred.

Between the beers and the almost accident, I was still in a state of shock. With the bright lights, commotion, and slow motion of everything all around me, I couldn't see or hear very much at all. But I could very much feel his *hard* body that not only shielded me, but was also pressed firmly against my leg, as he held me on top of him. But given the urgency of the situation at hand, I can totally understand why he would be so... tense, right now. At the moment, I was a little *tense* myself.

I could feel his shallow breaths on my face, as he cupped my cheek with his hand. A hand that was surprisingly warm, considering that it was chilly tonight, after days of pouring rain. This man just stared into my eyes with an intensity that looked vaguely familiar, but I could hardly see straight. But what I could see was his forehead rippled with anxiety. *He was worried.*

"Are you alright?" He whispered, close to my ear. I didn't recognize his voice, but it had warmth to it, with a slight rasp.

"I think so… I...I don't know," I muttered.

Just then, he slowly sat us both up from in-between the cars we were nestled under, and helped me up to my feet. We both were standing now, with his front to my side as I looked around at the commotion. He held me closely, with his arm around my waist supporting my body. I took a deep shuttering breath as I looked back towards him, but I still couldn't see his face clearly. I could only see the front of his cap and the hoodie that covered much of his face. I started to wipe my eyes with my arm, but it made things worse, and my vision became even more blurred.

"Can you stand?" He whispered, close to my ear, and I nodded as he slowly released me. After a few moments of standing on my own, realization began to dawn on me that I could have been hit by this massive truck. *I am such an idiot!* I just closed my eyes and thanked God again, that I was still alive. Looking over at the huge truck, parked awkwardly in the middle of the road, was as terrifying as when it was coming towards me, head on. I then felt a shiver run down my spine at the thought, and then I heard my friends.

They were yelling my name and as their voices grew closer to me, I then turned in the direction of the familiar voices. I then called back to them, as I unclearly saw them rushing towards me. "Oh my God, Jessica, are you alright?" Amber screeched.

"What the hell is wrong with you, Jess? Why did you run into the street?" She cried, wiping at my arms and face.

"You ran into the street. Why Jess?" Tracy asked.

As they bombarded me with questions, I took a few shaky breaths and looked around to see a small crowd gathering around us. I needed to rinse my eyes, the particles in them from the fall made my vison entirely too blurry, and I could barely see anyone clearly at all. As I began to look around, I could vaguely see everyone that was near us, except the one I was looking for. "Where is he?" I whispered, before turning back around to my friends.

"Who? Who are you talking about?" Sherry asked, perplexed.

"The guy... the guy who saved me?" I muttered to her.

"When the truck moved, we saw only you standing here. I didn't see a guy or anyone else. Who was he?" She asked, looking even more confused.

"I... I don't know." I stated, really feeling like an idiot. I didn't ask him one single question, but he managed to ask me two, while saving my life.

"This must be him," my friend, Tracy, announced. We all turned to look to where she was pointing, and there was a huge man approaching us. Sherry turned her head back to me after she saw him, and grabbed my hand.

"Is that him?" She asked me, as I saw the chubby man in the red hat approaching us.

"No, it's not," I snapped, starting to feel pissed off. I knew I wasn't going crazy.

I knew a man had saved me, and I knew he was somewhere out here. But I also knew that they would never believe me, just like the last time. I could hear an ambulance nearby, and I was glad, because I needed them to rinse my eyes ASAP.

"Excuse me, but are you alright?" The man asked, with a thick southern accent. The man who was driving the truck was the man standing before me, with panic in his voice as he spoke.

"Yes, I'm alright," I muttered, confused about it all. *I knew someone saved me.*

"Oh good, thank God. I am so glad I didn't hit you... it was a very close call," he exhaled. But I couldn't focus, because I needed to find the man who saved me. But I knew if he didn't want to be found, he wouldn't be. It was always on his terms when I saw him, always.

"I'm glad that you didn't hit me, too. Did you see who pulled me out of the way?" I asked, hoping he could confirm my scattered thoughts.

"No, I just tried to swerve out the way myself. I didn't see anything or anyone after I spotted you in the road," he stated.

"So you *didn't* see a man pull me out of the way?"

He shook his head, and I nodded as I saw the paramedics approaching me. I glanced over at my friends, who all wore the same expression. I could tell by the creases in their foreheads, that they all probably thought I was too drunk or just plain crazy. Maybe I was, darting out into traffic like that, putting myself at risk of getting hit.

I released Sherry's hand, before walking over to sit on the curb, and put my head in between my legs. I knew no one would believe me, but I knew what I saw and what I felt. Someone had saved me, and I think it was the same man who was watching me.

A few days after that whole ordeal, I'd decided to cut my losses and move out of the house ASAP. I was originally going to stay in the house until a few weeks after graduation, but decided against it. I needed to get away from that area, because it just didn't feel right staying there now, too much had happened and I wasn't going to prolong the inevitable any longer.

After securing my apartment and moving my start date up for my new job, I was beyond thrilled. Those next few weeks were good, all was calm. There were no more appearances from my supposed stalker or any more incidents of me being too drunk to function.

I was very glad that I was able to be moving on from it all, one mile at a time. It was such a great feeling to glance in my rearview mirror and see my *then,* while looking ahead and seeing my *now.* I was on the way, to a new beginning that was waiting for me... once I got there.

Chapter 6

A week later...

I had so many things going on in my life. I was now a college graduate, had fully moved into my new apartment, and was starting my new job in three days. It was such a great time for me, that I literally could not stop smiling. My family had flown in from Michigan, for my graduation and I was elated to see them. We had fun at dinner, and spent an extra day together before they flew back out.

My parents are wonderful parents and I was very lucky to have them. I missed them so much already, and they'd just left. They always made me feel as if I was their top priority, even though I wasn't living at home anymore, and I did the same in return. My father was such a great guy; he was into fishing, grilling and extensive home repairs. My mother was the complete opposite, she was very outspoken and the adventurous type. How the hell they ended up together still boggled my mind, but there was a delicate balance between them, and it was special.

I always hoped that I would have a special kind of love one day, but until I did I had my dad. I was and always would be; a daddy's girl. Because he was my hero. He worked so hard over the years, to ensure that I wouldn't have student loans hanging over my head for the next twenty years. He'd paid all of my tutoring and college expenses, and bought me my grey Camry in my sophomore year.

After I'd told him about a so-called "friend" of mines nauseating experience of being watched one night, when she was walking home from the library. He then decided to get me a car, to ensure that I didn't have to walk home late at night alone anymore, and be afraid. I didn't want to tell him that there was no friend, and that it had actually happened to me. But I didn't want to cause him to panic, and I felt as if I had things under control, somewhat.

I decided a long time ago, that I would not accept any jobs offers near campus, and move away from the area as soon as I graduated. A decision was made. My father always understood my stubbornness, while supporting my decisions, and I loved him for that. He and my mother always provided for me and I loved them so much, we have a great relationship.

I found myself smiling as I thought about my parents, while downing my glass of wine, and choosing a dress out of my closet. *I was going out tonight.* I deserved to have some fun before I started my new job this week, and I would. I knew that my old roommates were having a get together at the house tonight. I really didn't want to go, but I promised Sherry that I would at least stop by for a bit.

I didn't have anything to worry about, I didn't live there anymore nor would I have to deal with the aftermath of the madness that would occur. So I'd go to the "get-together" for a little while at least. *What's the harm in that?*

It was the last week that they would have the house, so that meant that they were having a party. The house was a good twenty miles away from my new residence, but I knew if need be, I could stay in a hotel for the night, if I didn't feel like the drive back home.

Because there was no way, not under any kind of circumstances, would I be staying another night in that house again. I was not interested in reliving any of those audible nightmares that I had to endure repeatedly, while living there.

The idea of getting drunk off of cheap beer was not appealing to me at all, so I opted for a glass of white wine at home while I dressed. But I haven't had dinner yet, so I needed to eat some food, once I got there.

I had no intentions of partying so hard that I passed out or got sick, being as though neither was my style at all. That kind of idiocy was for the idiots, not me. I'd rather do things my way and keep it simple and enjoy myself. I applied my makeup, slipped on my heels, zipped up my two-layered, silk-covered, laced pink and black dress, and was on my way. I really didn't feel like going to this party, but I did want to go and wish them all a farewell, and have a little bit of fun before I entered the real world of adulthood.

I had my own way of thinking and only followed my own rules, for my life. I am a twenty three year old woman with light blue eyes and long dark blond hair. I have always been told that I have a very pretty face, and that

I need to loosen up a bit more. But I don't listen to strangers and I definitely don't listen to my friends either. I only listen to me. I am 5'8" and I loved that I wasn't stick thin.

I have curves and I loved my body, no matter what society classified as beautiful, because I was born to be me. I've had only one boyfriend, and he was from back home in Michigan, and his name was Michael. We dated for three years, and it was nice. So nice that he was my first and only lover. I thought we were destined to be together, but after finding his massive porn collection, and another girl's panties in his room one day, I broke it off.

Luckily for me, I was only two weeks away from being shipped off to college, so I was able to mourn and sob in another city, and not drive my family crazy too much with my depression over the breakup. Because that's exactly what I did that first year away from home.

I mourned, heavily and it was terrible. Eventually I realized that it was a good thing to find out he was a jerk, better now than later. Since Michael, I had only gone on two dates during my whole four years in college. That didn't mean I didn't get countless offers, or pressure from my friends to do the casual sex thing, but I would always decline. I just didn't want or need the distraction, and to be honest, I wasn't that bored.

Two dates in four years, and both dates were disasters. They both looked like gentlemen, but were anything but. As soon as we ate dinner, both of them begged and pleaded for me to immediately have sex with them. One was literally rubbing his cock while groaning; obviously thinking that he was turning me on. *Umm, no!* The other couldn't keep his mouth off my ear, he was trying so hard to wind me up that it completely turned me *off*.

I only agreed to go on a date, to get to know them a little more. I didn't agree for them to get laid, but let them tell it... But those were college guys for you; most of them were all about having fun. I was hoping that some nice guys would come to the party tonight, but I wouldn't be surprised if none showed up. I had no clue where the hell they were all hiding. *"Hey, nice guys... Come out and play once in a while, would you!"*

I was now ten minutes away from the house, and it was so strange to be passing by my old college. Because now, I was a college graduate. I wondered if Professor Brennan was really leaving Morgan State, his fan club would be crushed.

They probably would begin cyber stalking the man, since most of them graduated. I giggled at my wayward thoughts, but all of that was no longer my concern, I just sincerely hoped he wouldn't leave the university.

He was such a good professor, and he had a master of science and he taught psychometrics. He was so accomplished to be so young. I always had a feeling that he was under thirty, and I was right, because I'd found out he was twenty-nine. He was a young professor who has only been a professor for five years.

This man had graduated high school at sixteen, and then went to Berkeley on a full scholarship, before attending grad school. I actually took the time to read his bio on the university website, when I was requesting my records to be mailed to my new house address. I almost wished I would have read it sooner, to have a little insight about my brilliant professor.

I would always remember Professor Brennan. Always. Regardless of his many accomplishment, he was still a man you couldn't forget too easily. In my opinion, he was what I considered to be a *real* man.

He certainly had the ambition of a man, and he was very handsome. But he had other attributes that I appreciated. His presence for one, and his way of thinking, and I really liked how his character and demeanor, were always intact. Those were just a few of the things that made him attractive to me.

But when I was his student, I had immediately blocked those thoughts out of my mind, for the last three years. But I wasn't his student anymore, and now my mind could roam guilt-free about sexy ass Professor Brennan, whenever I wanted too.

I turned the corner as the house came into view, to see that there were cars *everywhere*. There were some up on the side on the lawn, as well as some still running, with no one inside them, in front of the house. *What the hell?* Did I really consent to coming to *this*? Now all I wanted was a nice bath, another glass of wine, and maybe a good book by; Ramona Gray, to read.

I parked on the other side of the street, turned off my ignition, and found myself staring silently at the car in front of me as I took a few deep breaths. I then realized that I had a little buzz from the glass of wine I'd drunk, maybe because I'd only eaten breakfast today? I started to giggle as I reached for my purse to head inside.

My dress and heels now made me feel overdressed, for the ***rave*** that was now occurring before my eyes. If my best friend hadn't been in there, I would have just left. But I promised her I would come, and I needed to see her, even if just for a few minutes. But I already knew that it wouldn't take much to happen here, for me to be making a mad dash back home. I exited the car and crossed the street.

There were people all over the lawn and it seemed that *everyone* had a red cup, which I already knew was a bad sign. I walked up the concrete stairs, and ignored the whistling from a few guys, as I made my way into the crowded house. The house was *packed*. It has never been this crowded, ever. There were college kids everywhere, and I do mean everywhere. I could barely move.

It was as if I was at a concert, and I was in the first row trying to get to the back door. Bodies smashed on each other, some people were dancing and others were pushing and shoving one another, while others were jumping up and down. *O.M.G.*

This was just insane, and everyone smelled of beer and cigarettes. I suddenly felt claustrophobic and a little lightheaded, this was *not* my scene at all.

I couldn't believe that I had driven twenty miles for this. Instead of pushing further inside, I turned, and began pushing my way back out. I was not going to deal with this circus. After five minutes of being shoved, and having my ass groped by random hands, I finally made it back outside, and I practically ran to my car and slammed the door. I took a few deep breaths and wondered when the police would show up, because it really wasn't a question of *if* at this point.

This neighborhood had never been so *live*, and I was sure this party would be ending very soon. I pulled out my cell phone, knowing my best friend wouldn't hear hers, with the music as loud as it was, but it was worth a shot to try and call her. After four rings, her voicemail picked up. *"Hey, you've reached Sherry. Leave me a message and I will return.* -Beep

"Hey Sher. I'm outside, and I couldn't get in because the place is overcrowded. A warning would have been nice, but I'm leaving now. I can't do this, so we will have to catch up before you leave for Jersey tomorrow evening. Maybe I will stay in town at a hotel for tonight, possibly the Marriott. Call me in the morning, and I will see you for lunch, maybe around two? Love ya. Bye." -Beep

I started my car, and headed toward the nearest beltway, so I could find a hotel for the night. I had only ever stayed in one of the hotels closest to the campus, and it was so bad that I promised myself I would never stay there again. I drove five miles to the nearest hotel, which actually turned out to be the Marriott. This hotel was not in my budget, but I did have a credit card for emergencies, and I would classify this at an emergency.

Since I hadn't eaten any food before I started drinking, I was too buzzed from my "glasses" of wine to drive home safely. *Hmm, sounded good to me.* I just hoped that my father bought it. But truthfully the wine did have me a little off balance, so it was best not to attempt to drive the twenty miles back home. Especially when I'd only have to come right back in the morning to meet Sher.

My only hope was that I wasn't being watched while I was here in town. It was such a good feeling to not have the hairs on the back of my neck stand up, not once, since I'd moved. I felt as if I were free and also in the clear from all immature creeps. I gave my keys to the valet, and went inside the Marriott to get a room for the night.

As I headed to the front desk, I heard some music from the on-site lounge, and it sounded like jazz. After the couple in front of me walked away, I stepped up to the front desk and smiled.

"Hello, and welcome to the Marriott. How may I help you?" The receptionist asked.

"Hello, I need a room for tonight. A king size bed, non-smoking floor, and a late check-out please. Oh, and what time does your room service stop delivering?" I murmured, all in one breath.

"I see you are one to know *exactly* what she wants," a man stated behind me, but I somehow sensed recognition in his voice. I then turned around to see Professor Brennan standing there, with a smile on his face. I found my eyes involuntarily roaming down his body, as shock coursed through me. I'd never seen him like this, so relaxed and normal, and he wasn't wearing a suit. He had on blue jeans, and a white button shirt, with a dark blue blazer. He looked very nice, and he smelled good too.

"Um, hello, Professor Brennan." That was all I could say to him, since I was still in shock. *What was he doing here? Was he alone?*

"Hello, Jessica, how are you?" He asked smoothly.

"I am, fine," I said, swallowing, and finding my eyes roaming once again over his body. I knew in that moment, that this was a very bad time to be tipsy.

"Are you here for the jazz being played tonight?" He waved his arm toward the music that could be heard from where I stood.

"I guess you can say that, since I was just getting a room," I replied, before turning back to the lady. I handed her my credit card as she smiled, though I think it was more of a smile for him than me. He just seemed to bring that out of women, but I always found it be intimidating.

"Care to join me? I have a table reserved already," he asked. I nervously looked over at the lounge, and then back at him, and he smirked. *Oh God a dimple!*

"Professor, I don't think—" He interrupted me.

"Come on, Jessica. I'm staying here tonight as well, and we can catch up."

"Umm, I guess that's okay, for a little while at least."

I knew I didn't believe the words I was speaking. I knew this was wrong, so wrong. But I couldn't stop the desire clawing at me, to just be near him now. Since I wasn't his student anymore, I wouldn't be seeing him or talking to him about anything in the future. Truth be told, I missed his conversations, even if it was only about academia. I wasn't a part of his fan club, but I appreciated a real man when I saw one. Besides, at this stage in my life, I'd only seen two so far. My father and Professor Brennan.

"Okay, professor, I'll join you." I confirmed again, but mostly to myself. It seemed as if I needed to answer the question again and again, to myself. *Jazz with Professor Brennan, is this right?*

"Excuse me, Miss Moore?" The receptionist murmured. I then turned to her, and she handed me my room key and credit card. "So room seven thirteen is ready for you. Room service is open until midnight, and we have a free breakfast set-up from eight until ten, in the breakfast area to your left. If you need anything else, please call us," she stated, and I nodded to her.

"Thanks," I replied.

"Excuse me, do you have any packages for room seven thirty six?" Professor Brennan asked her, and I felt the color drain from my face. *We were booked on the same floor?* What are the odds of *that* happening? I took a deep breath as she handed him a small envelope, which he'd then slid in his suit jacket, and then he turned to me with a smile.

"Shall we?" He asked.

"Sure," I said.

"Great, and by the way, Jessica… I feel the need to reiterate that *you* are no longer *my* student, and I am no longer your professor. So with that being said, you can call me Thomas. My name is Thomas Vincent Brennan, and you, Jessica Moore, look very beautiful tonight." He stated, as his eyes roamed over my pink and black dress and black heels.

He didn't linger at my body too long, because his eyes were back on my face in seconds. I knew I was flushed and dazed, this was just all too much. I was only just thinking about him on the drive over, and now he's here and we're about to go to a hotel lounge together.

"Yes, I see. Thanks, you too," I muttered warily.

What was I saying? Was I even making sense? He then held up his forearm and I looked down at it for three long seconds, while his hand rested over his ribcage, as he silently awaited my compliance. I then entwined my arm into his and we then headed in the direction of the lounge.

I didn't know about him, but I knew what I needed right now, and that was a drink... or two.

Chapter 7

As we headed towards the lounge, the only thing that I kept repeating in my head was; this is *not* a date, this is *not* a date, this is *not* a date. The chanting was only a distraction, until I could make some sort of sense of my current predicament. Was this just a coincidence, or was it more?

Maybe this could just really be as simple, as a coincidence, us both being at the same place at the same time? Ugh, I sounded so stupid when I couldn't think straight. So at that moment, I decided to not over-think things at all, not until I at least had a shot. The lounge was a nice size, almost the size of a medium-sized restaurant.

There was a small stage in the center of the room, near the back. There the band was playing and a nice looking African-American woman who stood in front of a mic, singing tones and melodies. The way she sang without actually using words, had me immediately entranced. She sounded so erotic, and the soft sounds of the live band flowed so lovely around her intoxicating voice.

The music overall was very enchanting, and I immediately knew that I'd enjoy myself tonight. I looked on as Thomas led me to his private booth near the front of the stage. Then and only then, did he remove his arm from around mine. He then placed his hand on the small of my back, ushering me forward as I nervously glanced up at him.

I entered the booth and scooted over, and he then sat inside the booth and moved closer to me. I glanced at him again and we both smiled at each other, as I set my purse on the table and looked around this place. It was a very nice setting, and had a romantic feel to it. It didn't feel like a cheap looking hotel lounge at all. The ceiling had sparkling lights hanging down, and there were tables and booths surrounding a small dance floor in front of the stage, where a few couples were swaying to the music.

All the tables were filled, with people actively listening to the music. It was like a sold out concert in here, filled to capacity. They all seemed like they were almost in a trance, from the jazz they were hearing. The same kind of trance you'd witness at a poetry reading, the people were always so in-tuned with their surroundings, literally.

Just like they were tonight, in this place, with the soft jazz playing. I actually liked it here, and that was odd, because I never liked most of the clubs that my friends dragged me out to.

"I like it here, it has a very relaxing atmosphere," I murmured, while looking over at him and suddenly realizing just how close he was, when he faced me. I've never been this close to him, I could actually smell his cologne. A long moment passed as we gazed at each other, with no words spoken.

"I agree. I come here when I need to do exactly that, relax and enjoy myself," he murmured, as his eyes lowered to my lips and then back up to my eyes. "This group plays here once every month, and I try to make it each time," he finally replied, after clearing his throat.

"I would too, if I had known about them. This music is so good, I really like it," I smiled, ignoring the butterflies fluttering in my stomach.

"Maybe later you'd join me for a dance then?"

"Hmm, maybe, but I need a drink first," I responded. He then leaned forward and pressed a button on the side of the table, and a waiter appeared shortly after.

"Mr. Brennan, nice to have you back, sir. What can I do for you tonight?" The waiter eagerly asked. *He really is a regular here.*

"Is champagne alright, Jessica?" He asked me, gauging my answer. *Isn't champagne for celebrating?*

"Sure, but I would love to add a shot of whiskey though," I stated. His eyebrows rose in surprise, and I smiled at him. He then nodded to me, as he turned back to the waiter.

"A bottle of Champagne, and *two* shots of whiskey."

"Yes, sir, right away." The waiter scurried off, as Thomas turned back to me. I could see the question written all over his face, without him even asking.

"My Dad always says that whiskey calms you down, and even though champagne sounds amazing, I knew I needed a shot of the *calm* that only whiskey can deliver," I offered.

"I see, well your father definitely knows what he's talking about. But there are *other* ways of achieving that *calm* you desire, without the consumption of alcohol, Miss Moore," he stated, and winked at me. I knew now that he was indeed flirting with me, yet again.

"So, how have you been, Professor?" I asked him as I tried to ignore the warmth I was beginning to feel between my legs.

"You aren't going to stop calling me professor, are you?" He chuckled.

"I like it, actually. In and out of the classroom," I'd stated, before I could catch myself. *What the hell.*

"As you wish. To answer your question, I am doing well. I'm glad that the school year is over, and my academic vacation has officially started," he replied.

"Wow, that's great. So, are you traveling some, or are you staying close by?" I didn't know why I asked him that, but I really wanted him to answer my question. No matter how invasive it was.

"A little of both, but that may change in the

foreseeable future." He smirked at me. I found myself taking a deep breath, to calm my nerves and unfiltered mouth.

"I wish I could have had more of a break, to at least travel a little, before I start my new job. Unfortunately I didn't get much free time, but that's partially my doing. So for me, I went straight from college, to working full-time. I start on Monday, and I'm so excited," I beamed.

"That's great, Jess, I am very proud of you." He stated.

"Thank you so much, for everything, Professor."

"My pleasure. So, if you *could* travel, where would you go?" He asked. The waiter then approached us with our drinks. He began to set down the bucket holding the bottle of Champagne, and the two shots of whiskey. Meanwhile, I was thinking of my answer to his question. *Where would I want to travel?*

"Jessica?" He called my name, and I looked over to see him staring at me.

"Oh, sorry, I was still thinking of where I wanted to travel. There are so many places, I can't narrow it down to just one," I murmured.

"I understand. I was going to ask if you've eaten dinner."

"Um, well, not exactly."

"Okay, neither have I. So, we'll eat then, okay?"

"Yes, I can eat." Once the waiter returned with a menu, he then started to order a few dishes for us. It took me by surprise that two of the dishes he ordered, were my favorites. How was it that we had the same taste in food, when he seemed so worldly?

I always thought he probably ate raw fish and alligator, or something else exotic. But he actually liked chicken parmesan, and steak and potatoes, and so did I. He'd put in the order for those entrées, and then the waiter had left.

"That was amazing," I murmured, while shaking my head at him.

"What was?" He asked.

"You chose two of my favorite meals without even asking me."

"Well, maybe it's my lucky day," he stated, as he winked at me.

"Maybe it is," I giggled, as I reached for the two shots, handing him his. I held mine up, thinking of what to say. "Hmm… what shall we toast to, Professor?"

"How about we toast to a great future?" He offered.

"Okay, to a great future," I repeated, and we clinked our shot glasses, as we both threw back the liquid fire. I then blew out a long breath afterwards, as it was surely needed.

"You okay?" He asked. Obviously the whiskey did nothing to his throat, since he was so calm as if he'd drank water.

"Yes, I am fine. I would like a glass of champagne now."

"I never took you for much of a drinker, Miss Moore." He chuckled, as he reached for the champagne bottle in the ice bucket, and started to fill both our glasses.

"I'm not. I mostly prefer a glass or two of wine periodically, but sometimes, a gal needs a shot of whiskey," I teased. He chuckled at my playful demeanor as he handed me my glass, and I smiled at him sweetly.

"I'm guessing this is one of those times?" He arched a brow.

"Well, aren't you clever? You don't know

too much about me, professor, so let's not presume. I don't presume to know you, but if I'm permitted, I can learn," I admitted boldly, the liquor was already making me braver than I really was.

"Okay, I get it, but I can learn as well. Keep in mind that I am fully aware, of your learning capabilities, Miss Moore."

"Oh, well you'd do well to keep in mind that, I am also fully aware of your teaching capabilities, Professor Brennan."

"You're very intelligent as well as entertaining, Miss Moore. In and out of the classroom," he stated, and clinked my glass. We both then drank some of our champagne, while our eyes stayed locked on each other's.

As much as I was trying to stay in control of things and not over-think this *non-date* with him, I felt as if I was completely out of my league. But I couldn't deny that I was having a great time, just being with him, in this way. So, I sat back and got comfortable, as I let the sweet sounds of jazz take me away, and away I was taken, with my professor right next to me.

Chapter 8

"Jessica?" He murmured, and I turned from looking at the stage, to look over at him.

"Hmmm?"

"So, back to the previous question, where would you like to travel?" He asked, as he looked at me intensely.

"Oh, I don't know, Thomas. I would love to visit Italy one day, and maybe Australia and St. Croix," I replied absentmindedly and he smiled.

"Those are very good choices, and I think you'll get to visit them all one day. Sooner than you think." He replied, while taking another sip of his champagne.

"Oh yeah, how? I don't have the resources for that kind of traveling, not to mention the time or companionship. I wouldn't want to go alone and all my friends are leaving, and I won't have anyone here with me after tomorrow," I sighed, and looked back at the stage.

"You'll have me. You'll always have me," he muttered. Unsure if I'd heard him right, I turned to look at him, as my eyes widened. I was dumbfounded, at the words that came out of his mouth. Not at the validity of his words, but the instant response of that kind of a statement. It had actually made me breathless, as I gasped. In some strange way, I felt as if this was *more* than just a casual dinner between acquaintances.

Just being with him, in this way, seemed like it was... more. I felt like I was entering the outer realms of our very limited relationship. It almost felt like an initiation to the other side that has now been approved and activated. The fraternizing issues were no longer a factor, because I was out of school now. So the truth is, there was no limits standing between us now. *But would I allow anything to happen between us? Did he want something to happen?* I didn't want to think about it, so I took a deep breath and decided to just... see what happens.

"You okay, Jess?" He asked, concern etched on his face.

"Oh, Professor, let's dance," I blurted out. The alcohol had loosened my tongue and I wanted to just do what I felt like doing, which at the moment was to dance.

"Okay," he muttered, and helped me out of

the booth. As we made our way to the dance floor, I found myself rambling about my night. I'd told him about that insane party, and my last minute plans to stay in town tonight. I was trying to do something I normally wouldn't do with men, and that was to live in the moment.

As soon we reached the dance floor, I turned towards him, and immediately stopped talking. I stood there, thinking that maybe this wasn't a good idea after all. But before my nerves could get the best of me, he roped his arm around my waist, pulling me to him. My breath hitched as my mouth parted, and he smirked at me.

"It's alright, Jess, to come closer. I've got you," he uttered, as he stepped closer to me. I placed my hand on his shoulder as he grabbed my other hand. *Oh god.* We just stood there, motionless, while breathing each other in.

We were now face-to-face, closer than we've ever been, while our bodies almost touched. There was maybe half an inch between us, and it was too much for me to handle. I felt like his touch and his scent were making me even tipsier, than I already was. *I could get drunk off of him.*

He continued to stare at me, with a thirst in his eyes so intense, it was making me tremble. We began to sway to the music as we gazed at each other, and I wondered what he was thinking. For two songs our bodies swayed to the soft jazz, in the semi-darkened room. There we were, growing closer and more comfortable with one another. By the second song, my head ended up on his chest, and his nose buried in my hair.

By the time the third song started, my arms were wrapped around his neck, as I ran my fingers through his hair. I wanted him, and I wanted him badly and I wasn't alone. He was in the zone himself, as both his hands gripped my waist, pulling me closer to him, as if I was his prey. I would see his eyes lower periodically, to my lips and then he'd pulled me even closer to his *hard* body. I've always had an overwhelming desire for him, but I always put all my energy into fighting it. But now, I don't think I had any more fight left in me.

I didn't know if I could resist this man, if he actually wanted more with me. I couldn't believe that my body was reacting to him, in such an overpowering way. I guess I could lie to myself all I wanted too, but the body *never* lies. He was hard-pressed against my stomach, and I was soaking wet.

After we danced to the third song, we then left the lounge, and headed toward the elevators. I think both of us were tipsy and insanely aroused, but I was no longer fighting it. *I wanted him to fuck me, tonight.* We rode up to the seventh floor in silence, but the dirty thoughts that passed between us, were very obvious. I still wasn't sure what could be done about it, he was so out of my league. But I was willing to find out, I think.

I was already feeling the emptiness that was now consuming me, since we'd left the dance floor. A few minutes ago he'd released me on the dance floor and grabbed my hand, and I felt my world slowly crashing, just from the detachment of his body. I wanted more, and he wanted more too. I could feel it when we danced, he was pressed so close to me, that I could feel his erection on my stomach.

He reached over to hold my hand, and I let him, and he exhaled a breath. The elevator pinged as we reached the seventh floor, where we both had rooms for the night. We walked out of the elevator, and he'd made a left, while still holding my hand. I quickly realized that I hadn't looked at the sign near the elevator, to see if they were walking on the right side of the hall. As we walked down the hall, I looked around at the numbers, and saw that they were going up and not down. A moment later I realized why, as we came to a complete stop. We now stood hand in hand in front of a room, his room... room seven thirty six.

"Jess?" He murmured, as I desperately tried not to over-think things, but that seemed impossible. I was the hornist I'd ever been in my life, but it was still a battle of wills. *Could I do this? Would I do this? Should I do this?*

"Yes?" I replied, breathing deeply, trying to fight the desire clawing at my soul.

"You okay?" He asked. I knew why he was asking me if I was okay. He needed to know it if I was too intoxicated, from the few drinks I'd had. Yes, I was a little tipsy, but the food we ate had assisted in keeping me leveled. I was only drunk with hunger, hunger for him.

"Yes, I'm okay... more than okay," I responded, as I reached into my purse, looking for the key to my room. I knew that I didn't need it, but I needed to distract myself for a moment. Because we were standing in front of *his* room, and I wasn't sure what I should do at this point. As I pulled out my room key from my purse, he quickly snatched it from my hand. As he moved closer to me, backing me up against his door.

"Ugh, professor—" I started to say, but my words left me as he stepped even closer to me, completely invading my personal space. I looked up into his eyes, and they were so intense. I was used to his intensity, but not *this* kind of intensity. This intensity was new, intoxicating, and arousing even. I wanted him, but I never imagined that he wanted me too.

"Jessica, I want to... I need you," he muttered, close to my mouth, as I tried to remember to breath. *In... Out..... Breathe In..... Breathe Out, Jessica.*

Even though I didn't have much experience with men, I could tell that he wanted to kiss me, as his eyes had lowered to my lips again. I slowly raised my hands toward him, and ran them up his chest, as he exhaled. I could feel his warm breath on my lips, as he leaned closer to me. I tried to mentally prepare myself for this kiss; a kiss I had always wanted, but never ever thought I would get. But it didn't happen. *The kiss didn't happen.*

What did happen made my eyes widen in shock and in fear, when I suddenly heard a loud "BEEP" and then a click. As the door to his room was being pushed opened, by his hand. OMG. *Was this really happening to me right now?* I turned and looked behind me, and into his room. Before I turned back to him, eyes wide and flushed. He smirked and took my hand, and walked inside his room.

Once he was inside, he turned and looked at me, and then down at my heels. I was still standing in the hall, right over the threshold. I had a choice to make. I could either cross the threshold, or run to my room like a scared little girl. Even though I was nervous as hell, I knew this was a once in a lifetime opportunity, happening right here and now. I had never been with another man since my first, Michael. So I was a bit hesitant, on my next lover being my professor. But he wasn't my teacher anymore and I now lived twenty miles away from here.

So why not him? I swallowed and took a step forward, entering his room, with the door slamming behind me.

Chapter 9

Jessica had no clue that her car had not only been bugged, but it also had a tracking device planted inside. For the last several months, he ensured that he *always* knew her whereabouts and also her destinations. He had the tracker placed on her car for her protection at first, since there had been a few reported incidents around campus. But he quickly realized that he wanted to know more about her, than just where she was located. He wanted to be able to hear her voice, and hear her talk about something other than academia. He needed more, and was determined to enhance his surveillance on her, and planted the bug.

Who was he becoming?

After he'd bugged her car, he could hear her talking anytime he wanted to now. She would talk on her phone to her friends, while she drove around town. As a result of the planted bug, he knew about the party she would be attending, days before. She was talking to her best friend, Sherry, on speaker-phone while driving last week.

So on the night of the party, he knew that she was on her way to town, to see her friends. He knew she was in route because of the tracking device, he'd planted on her car. But as she drove into town, she had no clue that he was right behind her, following at a distance. He wanted her safe, he needed her to be safe, but that's not all that he wanted. He wanted so much more; he wanted to protect her, to love her, and cherish her. She meant more to him than any other woman he'd been with in his entire life. He knew very early that he'd never meet anyone else like her again, within that first year of meeting her, actually.

The more time they spent together being professor and student, the more he found himself falling for her. He loved everything about her, everything he could see, and everything he couldn't wait to see. He knew his feeling wouldn't change for her, he'd come to that conclusion a very long time ago. By the second year of her being his student, he knew he was madly in love with her. He only wished she would catch up to him, and soon.

So after he'd heard the voicemail she'd left for Sherry, while outside the party at her old house. When she'd stated that she was staying in town tonight, and most likely at the Marriott, he was elated. This was his chance. To not only see her again, but to also let her know how much she meant to him, in some way that wouldn't scare her off.

There was no chance that he would miss this opportunity that had presented itself. But if he didn't make it in time, he wouldn't be able to get everything ready. He knew he only had a limited window to react, and he needed to hurry.

***

He honestly didn't think he would get there in time, because she was already leaving the house party. But he drove like a mad-man to get there before her, and luckily he did. He'd made it to the Marriott, and set things up to look as if he'd already been staying there.

Courtesy of their overly helpful concierge and the thousand dollar tip, he'd split between that same concierge, and the flirtatious receptionist. He never spared any expense when it came to Jessica, and that would never change.

Everything went smoothly at the reception desk when Jessica had arrived, a little too smoothly, as if it was all real. The staged package for his room, which was suggested by the concierge, was a very nice touch. The envelope he was handed only held his room key, after she'd reserved her room, putting them on the same floor, as planned.

After giving the receptionist a slight nod, they proceeded to the lounge. That innocent nod of the head was anything, but innocent. It confirmed what she was supposed to ensure happened next, while they listened to the jazz band in the lounge. Given the urgency of things, he was very impressed that they were able to pull this off. They were a bit skeptical at first, but he had no time to waste.

He'd explained to them that he and his girlfriend were role playing, and he was her "professor" for the night. Which was the first thing that popped up in his head. Surprisingly, after hearing that bogus explanation, they obliged to help him. Now it was his turn to bring it home, and he intended to do just that. He watched her finish her first glass of champagne, and then her second, and he wondered if she was already hammered.

She said she didn't drink too often and that she needed one tonight, and maybe she did. Once the food came, they both ate a little from each plate, as if they normally did this together all the time. He was pleasantly surprised at her ability to eat in front of him. Most women were scared to death to eat in front of a man, but not Jessica Moore. He watched her out the corner of his eye, as she began to move her body, to the sweet sounding music.

He knew he would ask her to dance later, if she wasn't too tipsy. The band was now taking a short break, while they talked. He didn't realize how much time had passed, because he was having such a good time with her. He really didn't want the night to end. Thomas was a man who was as committed and devoted to Jessica, as if they were a couple already. She was so titillating to him, from the very moment he first met her, three years ago in his orientation.

She was the only student to ask him questions on that first day, and they were very good questions at that. Her inquisitive mind and audacious and fearless demeanor in academia were very appealing to him, not to mention her breathtaking beauty. He knew almost immediately that he liked her, very much.

His interest in her began to bloom, and the more time they spent together, it intensified even more. But regardless of how he felt, he knew he had to wait until both of them were no longer bound by the laws of the University.

He needed to protect not only himself, but her future as well, and he did. But as the years passed, he couldn't stop thinking about the possibilities. The possibilities of them being more than what they were, and he desperately wanted to explore those options for the two of them. Those thoughts always sat dormant in the back of his mind, causing him to become frustrated and overeager to get closer, to her.

He always wondered if he would actually have the chance to be with her after she graduated, and it was happening right now, in this very moment. This was his chance to do something he'd often dreamed about doing with her, for years. To just enjoy a consensual night out, with a little dinner and maybe some dancing. Away from everyone and without the pressure of the university's fraternizing policies, or the demands of her other classes hanging over either of their heads.

He really didn't need to wander too far into his head right now, but it was a slippery slope with the way she looked tonight. He couldn't stop looking at her, wanting, needing, craving to just, touch her. Everything he wanted was sitting right next to him, looking at him in a way that took his breath away. But he was very distracted while with her, and tense.

He was terrified that he would somehow scare her off, and had to make sure that didn't happen, so he proceeded with caution. She had no idea of the power she held over him, and his body. The proof of that power continued to twitch between his legs, proving to be *harder* than he'd ever imagined it could be. He knew how crazy things had become, regarding his feelings for her, but he didn't know if it made any sense at all. Was it really possible to be in a relationship with someone, without them knowing about it?

Who had he become?

She was the only woman to get him so turned on that he couldn't think straight, or could barely concentrate on anything else. If she only knew, the true power she held over the man sitting next to her. His mind, body and soul were all focused on her, only her. At times he even had trouble breathing while they sat side by side.

She was so close to him, too close. He could actually reach out and touch her... kiss her... take her. He was having a very *hard* time with the fact that with each intake of breath, he could actually smell more of the one he craved, desperately. She smelled so damned good to him, so sweet and innocent, and it took all of his self-control to not react. Her fragrance was so intoxicating, her presence was all-consuming, making his hunger for her take him to place of *no* return.

The man was going crazy, his mind continued to race as he could already envision tasting her. He didn't know how much more he could take, he was so close to snapping. He couldn't wait anymore, he needed her. He would had devoured her on the table before them, not giving a damn who saw. Once she'd asked him to dance, he cleared his throat and quickly readjusted himself and escorted her to dance floor.

He had never been so anxious before, as if to pass out. But as they made their way to the dance floor, his heart was thundering so hard he'd thought he might. A few songs later and he was in another realm, as her hands tightened around his neck. This was so much more than he could handle right now, but it was all that he longed for.

An intimate touch, a merging of their bodies... her gaze fixed on his as he held her close. He found himself grasping her waist even closer to him, pressing himself into her as she trembled against him.

He needed her to feel what she does to him, and once a soft moan escaped her, he knew the game was over. She wanted him. He didn't waist another second as he pulled her off the dance floor, and towards he elevators. While one thing continued to plague his mind. Would she actually say yes to a night with him... and a

lifetime?

Chapter 10

As the door slammed shut, I realized that I was now fully inside his room. I looked down at our entwined hands, exhaled, and looked back up to him. He began to pull me towards him, and I let him. As our bodies met, he began to dance with me, as if we were still on the dance floor in the lounge, with his arm sliding around my waist.

We had good dancing symmetry as we moved as one, and it was so mind boggling that I felt as if I was drifting. Our bodies slowly swayed to the silent sounds of our breathing, as he gazed solely at my face, and I gazed at his. I couldn't read his expression, but I didn't feel the urge to run away from him, so I allowed myself to calm down. I was glad that I wasn't settling for just anyone, who in my eyes, didn't even qualify for me.

Professor Brennan was the only other man whom I'd even considered to be a man, other than my father. My hands slowly slid up his chest, and around his neck, as we slowly moved against each other. *He smelled so dammed good.*

His arm tightened around me, and I gasped near his lips. His nice lips, that I've wanted to suck on since I met him. His top lip was thin, but his bottom was a little thicker, and they looks so soft.

"Thomas?" I muttered, close to his mouth.

"Yes, Jessica?" He whispered huskily. I had never heard this tone from him before. He sounded so dark and dangerous and I felt my body clenching, as I began to pant.

"Please," I begged, as I felt my nipples hardening even more, as I subtly arched my back into him.

"Please what?" He questioned.

"Touch me," I responded.

"I am, you want more?" He asked me.

"Yes, much more." The swaying stopped, and was replaced with slow shallow breaths between the both of us, as he looked through me. He raised his hand, ran his fingers through my hair, and I closed my eyes as he tilted my head back, so that his lips were directly leveled with mine.

"I've always wanted more, Jessica, always," he muttered, before his lips connected with mine. I was still reeling over his statement of always wanting more, but my world had literally stopped once he kissed me. His lips were soft and determined, he kissed me with so much passion it was hard not to return it. I heard a soft groan escape him, as his hands trailed down my back, until he reached my backside. As he squeezed both cheeks softly, his tongue entered my mouth, conquering mine.

My hands slid down his back and around, as I gripped his blazer, pulling him into me. Soft groans and whipped air, became a surround sound to me, as we continued to kiss. He then pulled away from me, taking a few steps back, while looking at me intensely. The both of us were slowly panting for air, as our eyes roamed over one another. I nearly gasped at the bulge in his pants that was seriously overwhelming my eyes, and my thoughts. By the time I looked back up at him, I saw that he'd taken off his blazer, and was now removing his cufflinks.

"Jess, you're not a virgin are you?" He asked.

"No, but I've only been with one other guy... and that was four years ago," I muttered, almost ashamed.

"Okay, good."

"Okay good? You don't think that's kind of... pathetic?" I asked, as my eyes fell to his now exposed chest. *Wow!* His abs were so cut, and his V was so in-depth. My God, he actually looked as good under his clothes, as he did over them.

"Of course not. I don't sleep around either. In fact, if it makes you feel any better... I've only been with two women," he stated with a smile. I found myself smiling back, but then my smile became laughter, and I couldn't help it. *Who was he kidding?*

"You've *got* to be kidding me, professor," I exclaimed, disbelieving him, and then I realized his face showed no sign of humor, and that he was actually telling me the truth. My laughter stopped, and my mouth hung open, as I gaped at him.

"But, but... most of the population at the college wanted you, including the faculty," I declared, incredulously.

"I don't take everything that's offered to me, Miss Moore. I have to want it too." He winked, and took off his shoes and socks, as I stood there frozen like a statue. His last statement had me flabbergasted, and it meant that he really wanted me, a lot.

"Are you alright? You look nervous?" He asked, as he walked toward me with just his jeans on, he was almost naked. My goodness, Professor Brennan was almost freaking NAKED!

"Um, no, I'm fine. Just a little taken aback from your words," I replied.

"I understand. Jess, we don't have to do anything right now if you're having second thoughts. I just—"

"Please, don't. I want to. Help me with my zipper, will you?" I muttered, as I turned around, my back to his front. I then heard my zipper being pulled down slowly, and then with a slight shimmy, my dress pooled on the floor. I heard his sharp intake of breath, then he groaned and I smirked. I had on a black sheer thong, and no bra, and all of sudden I felt very happy with my choice in that matter. I knew when I turned around to face him, that there would be no going back. He would see *me,* and have *me*...in any way he wanted. He was a man, an attractive man who I've wanted for years, and he wanted me tonight.

We both would give in to our desires, and I couldn't be happier or even more scared, than I already was. I took a deep breath, and when I turned around, his eyes didn't stray. They were locked on mine. He didn't glance at my body, as I thought he would. He just wrapped his arm around my waist, and lifted me up. He pulled my legs around his waist, and took long determined strides to his bedroom. His eyes never left mine. Once there, he laid me down and kicked off his pants, leaving his light blue boxer briefs on. He climbed over me and kissed me, as if he has been waiting years for it.

Our mouths twisted and turned in a slow erotic way that made me extremely hot and bothered. His hands were in my hair, pulling me further into him. My hands were on his back, as I kissed him with my very own passion. *Oh God, I wanted him so much.* The feeling of his hot skin on mine made me feel so grand, it was like a forbidden fantasy of mine was actually coming true.

His mouth moved to my neck, nipping and licking my skin, as his hand slipped under my back, slightly arching it, pushing my breasts closer to him. He looked like it was Christmas, as his eyes widened at the sight of my exposed breasts. He then kissed each one reverently, and began to suck hard on my left nipple, causing me to arch even more into him.

"Oh God," I cried out, as he moaned. He began to lick around my areola, long hard licks, as he teased my other breast with his fingers. As he blew on my moistened nipple, the coolness of his breath made me shiver, as his mouth now attended to my other breast. I found myself panting shaky breaths, when he started kissing around my stomach, slowly licking around my navel. As I ran my fingers though his hair, moaning softly, the more he kissed my body, like a man who was starved. He ran his nose up the center of my underwear, inhaling deep breaths, as if he was going under water, and I smiled down at him. He caught my smile, and sent one back.

"Why are you smiling?" He asked.

"Why are you?" I teased.

"I'm finally going to taste your pussy, and make you come for me. Case and point." He smirked.

"Such language, Professor," I teased, as he pulled down my underwear while he continued to look at me.

"You love calling me Professor. I will admit that I like it, too… in and out of the classroom," he winked, and slowly pulled my thong completely off.

He then ran his hands slowly up my legs, while gazing down at my moistened center, licking his lips. "Beautiful," he sighed, and I blushed as he looked back up to me. "Have you ever thought about me, in this way?" He asked, his voice hoarse with desire.

"Of course I have," I panted. "You're the sexiest man I've ever seen," I stated too quickly, and both of us froze. "I…I'm sorry, I…"

"You what? You can't take it back now, Jess, and I don't want you to," he smiled.

"I've thought of *you* in this way, plenty," he stated wickedly.

"That's good to know, I think."

"You think?" He chuckled.

"Yeah, since you know... Oh GOD," I moaned loudly, as he sucked on my clitoris, and entered two fingers deep inside me as my insides hungrily clenched around him. My back arched off the bed, and my arms splayed over the sheets as I was taken from zero to a hundred in mere seconds.

"I think your body is confirming your words baby. Let me feel you," he said. His tongue licked and traced along my lower lips, taking time to show each one the proper attention it never had before. He groaned against me as he tasted me, paralyzing me in ecstasy, as he moved my hips closer. I felt his tongue lapping against the underside of my clit, before he'd suck on me softly, and then hard, as his fingers twitched deep inside me. *OH MY GOD!!*

I could tell he really enjoyed a trimmed cunt, as he hummed his appreciation while sucking on my lower lips, and lucky for me I had shaved today. I felt him licking my clit again, but more softly, and I moaned as my fingers reached his hair, pulling it softly. He pressed my knees wider, and I gasped at his sudden movement of my limbs. He then removed his fingers, and began to thrust his tongue inside me, twirling it around my inner walls, as I cried out, trembling.

"So good...mmm, baby." He moaned again and again. I was shuddering with every touch, with every lick, and every stroke that he delivered. I felt my entire body building to detonate off the face of the earth, and soon.

"Let go baby. I want to taste you... give it to me," he demanded, before he pushed two fingers back inside me, curving them, and I came... *hard*. He purposely moved his fingers slowly inside me, as I contracted around them. Successfully turning me into a greedy, and needy lover, as I moved against his face and fingers aggressively. I was desperate for more, and he gave it to me. There I was, screaming incoherently, gripping his sheets as my body arched and shook, while he sucked all that escaped me. I felt his tongue still lapping and licking the drippings he might have missed, as I whimpered in a semi-conscious state.

"My God...that was...the most...intense," I

panted, trying to catch my breath, as he pulled his boxers off. Then he grabbed a condom from his pants and wiped his face with a tissue from the box next to his bed. *Why is he prepared for sex, when he claims that he doesn't take what's offered to him?*

"What is it? Why do you have that face?" He asked, narrowing his eyes, as he rolled the condom on his impressive girth. *Um, wow, talk about a full package!*

"Nothing. I was just thinking about something," I stated, while staring at his cock. It was long and thick, and it looked perfect. But I knew it would hurt me.

"Well then, let me put your mind at ease." He climbed back on top of me, and he placed his elbows on either side of my head, as he looked into my eyes. I smiled, breathing deeply, and he smiled and ran his fingers through my hair. In that moment, I could tell that he really did want me. He looked like he couldn't believe he was about to enter me, and neither did I.

I was sure it would hurt, since he sopped up most of my moisture, but it didn't hurt as much as I thought, because he slowly pressed himself inside me. I closed my eyes, and absorbed him as best as I could. He took his time, inch by inch, and I happily took him and his delicious cock.

"You okay?" He asked a few times, as he gave me an inch, and then another inch. I nodded, not being able to speak, as I held onto his arms. He was only half way inside me, and then he pushed the rest of the way, and we both moaned loudly. Once fully inside, he stayed still, slightly trembling, as was I. "My God, Jess, you feel so good, baby."

I moaned my response as he slowly withdrew from me, all the way. To only re-enter me with a slow thrust of his hips, he repeated this motion again and then again, as we both groaned in pleasure. He took me over and over again, and just as I thought he would deliver another slow thrust, he would then surprise me with a hard, delicious thrust, causing me to cry out.

"Oh, God," I moaned.

"You like it hard, baby?" He asked.

"I like it anyway you want to give it to me, Professor," I groaned. He pulled back out and subtly his thrusts picked up speed and intensity. He pushed into me deeply, and at his own rhythm of pleasing me. We kissed while moaning into each other's mouths, as we began a tug of war over the other's body. Our bodies twisting and turning, our hands pulling and groping each other, as we savagely kissed.

Ecstatic moans and panting filled the air, as we opened ourselves up to one another. It was as if we couldn't get close enough, to one another. I felt so connected to him, in some odd way, as if we were together before. It actually helped me feel more than I've ever felt when having sex before, and give in to the passion between us.

I felt like the wind was being sucked out of me, as I approached the brink of yet another orgasm. As he sucked my nipple into his mouth, and used his teeth to pull on it, I arched my back, telling him I wanted more. He went and did the same exact thing to my other nipple, before coming back up and kissing me hard, and re-entering me again.

As our tongues and bodies merged, he and I both moaned loudly, from such a deep and gratifying penetration. This breach was not like the last, this was hard and unforgiving, and I loved every second of it. He was so far inside of me, it was as if he didn't want to come back out. I could tell from his small hard thrusts, that he would *not* be withdrawing from me too much.

He palmed my ass, pulling me closer to him as I arched my neck back at the fullness I felt. As he sucked and nipped at my neck while he groaned into me. He never hesitated to go deeper, so we both could enjoy the full benefit of his entire cock, being submerged in my contracting cunt. I was so full of him, a part of me felt as if he'd touch my core. I cried out until I was damned near hoarse, as he catapulted me and my entire body into a state of unimaginable bliss. I could feel him everywhere. Inside me, outside me, inside me again and again. *Damn, professor!!*

I couldn't complain, as he repeatedly stroked my g-spot, driving me mad with pleasure, while sucking, biting and kissing my lips. His slow, sharp thrusts took me higher, as he took me over and over. "Oh GOD, Thomas… OH GOD!" I yelled, as I dug my nails into his back, and he moaned loudly, gripping my hair. As my body tightened and released around him in a piercing death grip. *Yes, Yes, Yessss!!!*

I opened my eyes to see him biting down on my bottom lip while growling, as he continued to soak up my cries. He was flushed, sweat dripping from his brow, while he moaned and trembled, as pure pleasure took over his body.

"Oh, Jess...Jessica." he muttered and then groaned. He lowered his head, sucking my nipple into his mouth, making me dazed as I cried out.

"Oh Thomas, please, take me," I mewled, completely overwhelmed, and in complete surrender.

"Oh, Fuckkkkk," he roared, and began to thrust again, as his warm release entered me. We both just laid there, sweaty and sated, trembling and panting hard. He was still on top of me, and I could even feel the scorching heat of his seed through the condom.

"I think...that was the most...intense orgasm...of my entire life, Jessica." In honor of one of my favorite films, all I could do was reenact a scene, or a *word* if you will, from the film *Ghost,* and say "Ditto." Because I was rendered completely speechless.

Chapter 11

After we had sex, he went to the bathroom and disposed of the condom. When he came back, he pulled me into his arms, and we cuddled. He held me close, as I drew patterns on his chest, which was lightly covered in hair. We stayed that way for seconds, minutes, maybe even an hour, and I actually felt comfortable. *Maybe too comfortable.*

I could feel his nose buried in my hair, and he breathed so calmly, as if we'd done this a hundred times before. I felt sated, exhausted and somewhat dizzy, but I could still go another round with him, but I doubt that we would. The more I touched him, the more I found myself beginning to feel a little out of place. Being here with him like this, lounging around like old lovers. "I like that you said my name," he muttered into my hair.

"What do you mean?" I asked.

"When you came, you screamed out, Thomas," he replied.

"I did…It is a good name, but like I said

before, I like professor as well," I teased.

"Me too, Jess," he muttered, and placed long lingering kiss on my head. I kissed his chest, sat up, and looked at him, while he looked back at me. I could tell he was comfortable, oddly comfortable. But he looked so adorable, in his post orgasmic haze. I leaned forward and kissed his lips, lingering for a few moments, before pulling back. I then headed into the bathroom, unbashful, and completely in the nude.

When I came back out, he had his boxer briefs on, and he had gathered my clothes and heels on the chair near the dresser. I headed over and grabbed my underwear, and he came and took them from me, backing up with a wicked grin on his face.

"Where do you think you're going?" He asked, holding my thong behind his back, while grinning playfully.

"I was umm, going to my room now," I smiled.

"I want you to stay," he quickly stated, as he walked towards me, his eyes pleading.

"You do?"

"Yes, stay as long as you want," he told me.

"Are you going to give me my underwear?" I pursed my lips at him, challenging him.

"I don't think you need them," he smirked. As I reached for them, he held them up over his head. I jumped once to get them as we both started laughing at each other. He then moved closer to me, and his arm wrapped around my waist, and he kissed me. I kissed him back as his other hand cupped the back of my head, holding me close to his mouth. Our passionate kissing had quickly turned into something else entirely, as I was lifted and slammed against the wall.

We devoured each other's mouths. My hands tugging his hair, and his hands gripping my behind, spreading me open. I suddenly felt the tip of his cock, sliding against my wetness, as I moaned into his mouth.

"I told you... you don't need them, baby," he muttered against my mouth, as he tilted me towards his hardness, and I could feel the heat against me on contact. *Yes please!*

"I guess you were right, maybe I don't need them," I groaned.

"I won't object," he moaned, and in one long hard thrust, he pressed himself inside me, all the way to the hilt.

"Take me, professor. My God...take me," I moaned, pulling his hair and tilting his head. I kissed him hard, sucking his tongue, tasting him, while tasting me. I tightened my legs around him, pushing him deeper inside me, as he growled against my mouth.

"Just like that, baby," he groaned. There we were, up against the wall, kissing and humping like monkeys. Very loud moaning filled his room, and it couldn't be helped. Heated desire, skin slapping against skin, moisture dripping from the both of us, creating an intensity of pleasure unknown. We were treading dangerous territory, having unprotected sex like this... but it was too damn good to stop.

"*Goddamn*, I can't stop," he growled, as he pulled me closer, delving deeper, as I felt my body contracting around him.

"Don't stop!" I moaned loudly, as he grabbed my hair, entangling his hand into it and kissed me again. He kissed me deeply, moving my head around, controlling the kiss as I took all that he had to give. He pushed and pulled me up and down on him with his powerful hard thrusts. The sound of moisture and liquids building where our bodies met. I didn't want him to stop, this was too good.

"Oh yessss, mmm," I moaned, as I began to shatter around him. *Oh fuck!*

"Jess, are you on the pill baby?" He growled against my mouth. *I'm sorry...are you talking to me? I don't even know my own name at the moment.* "Jessica?" He growled.

"No, I'm not on anything... Oh God," I cried, as he grazed my neck with his teeth.

"I want you, to have my baby?" He whispered into my neck.

"What?" I cried. *What did he just say?*

"I want to come inside you. Tell me I can."

"I want to feel all of you, please," I moaned, as we kissed again.

"Oh Jess," he sighed, as he reached his release. It was like he'd literally left his body and reached the sun, as he released and released inside me. He moaned and gripped me tighter, kissing me, and licking me. I felt his scorching hot seed deep inside me, as he filled me up. When he looked up at me, there was something different about the intensity in his eyes. He looked as if he was just awakened from a very long slumber.

"Thomas... are you alright?" I asked him, as we tried to catch our breath, and he slowly pulled me off the wall. He kissed my lips, closed his eyes, and lowered his head to mine while breathing hard.

"I'm alright, Jess, more than alright."

"That's good, I was worried for a second," I suddenly realized that he was still inside me, and I moaned softly, as he moved to pull out of me.

"If you keep making those sounds, I won't pull out of you, baby." He groaned, and I could feel his semi-hard erection trying to regain life.

"Maybe we should rest a bit, you are quite overwhelming, Professor."

"So are you, Jessica." He then carried me over to the bed, and sat me on my feet. He then handed me my underwear, and grabbed his. *When did he take those off?*

"So, I can put my underwear back on now?" I teased.

"I think that would be wise, before I take you again," he smiled and winked at me. After a quick trip to the bathroom to clean myself up, I put my underwear back on and washed my face.

My makeup was a mess, literally. When I exited the bathroom, he'd grabbed a robe and was holding it open for me. I knew deep inside that I was ruined for other men, there will never be another one like Thomas. I smiled and slipped it on, tied the robe around me, and sat on his bed, and checked the time on my phone. It was already two in the morning and I was in utter shock.

"Are you hungry, Jess?"

"Yes, I think all that we ate earlier was depleted," I giggled.

"I agree. Get dressed."

"What? Where are we going?" I asked him, incredulously.

"It's a surprise. Now come on, let's get some food," he smiled.

"I hope we won't be gone too long, I need a few hours of sleep. I have a lunch date at two o'clock this afternoon," I murmured, as I started to get dressed.

"A lunch date. I hope it's with a woman?" He asked, with a little *base* in his voice.

"It is. Why Professor, you're not *jealous* are you?" I teased.

"I don't get jealous, because I don't share. I know who I want Jess, and that's *you*," he deadpanned. *Wow, ugh, o....k.*

"So, does that mean that you want to see me again?" I asked nervously, as he walked over to me, with my heels in his hands. He kneeled down in front of me, and held out my shoe as I placed my foot inside the heel. Then he held out the other, and I placed my other foot inside. He kissed my legs, and ran his hands slowly over both legs, mesmerized. Before he placed his face near my upper thigh and inhaled deeply, basking in the scent of us.

"Of course I want to see you again. Is that a problem?" He looked up at me, smiling. I smiled back, and shrugged.

"Um, maybe it is. I don't live around here anymore, I live maybe twenty miles away now."

"I have a few cars, and I do have something called a GPS, Jess," he said drily.

"Oh, so you're funny now." I walked away from him, but he pulled my hand, and gently tugged me towards him, holding me close.

"Sorry."

"For what?" I exhaled.

"For not being funny," as he pursued his lips I leaned forward and kissed them quickly.

"I want you, baby, and I hope you want me?" He then kissed my lips softly.

"I do, I always did," I admitted, and we kissed again, deeply. Then he grabbed my hand, and led me to the door. We headed out of the room, walking down the hall, hand in hand. He looked at me and smiled as we reached the elevator. He pressed the down button, before he leaned over and kissed me quickly. "Am I even going to see the inside of the room I booked tonight?" I asked and laughed.

"I seriously doubt it," he teased. We headed out of the hotel, and he handed the valet his ticket. As we stood there, I leaned on him and his arm tightened around my waist. "I know you're tired, baby," he muttered in my hair, as he inhaled deeply.

"I am. Very tired." I heard a car approaching, and saw it was a black Range Rover truck. He opened my door and I climbed inside, as he held me up from behind. Then we were off, to some unknown destination that was supposed to be a surprise for me. I ended up falling asleep after fifteen minutes on the road, and sometime later, I awakened to his voice and a kiss on my lips.

"Wake up baby, Jess?" I was tired, I could barely keep my eyes open. As he leaned in, and picked me up from the truck, I flickered my eyes opened.

"Where are we?" I asked, half sleep, as he started to walk towards a house, carrying me as if I weighed nothing.

"My house, baby. You can sleep while I make us something to eat," he said. A few minutes later, he was laying me down on a very soft bed, as he took off my dress, and covered me with a sheet and duvet. After he kissed my lips, I immediately fell back to sleep. That's all I could do, because I was so tired. I was exhausted, and my body was not capable of staying awake any longer. When I felt him pulling me closer to his warm, naked body. I turned and nuzzled into him and just enjoyed the feeling of being in his arms, if only for a night.

Chapter 12

I awakened hours later and smiled to see that I was still wrapped his arms. I looked around, and slowly realized that we were no longer at the hotel. *He really did bring me to his house, but why?* I slowly moved his arm and went to find the bathroom, which was right off the master bedroom we were in.

This bathroom was the size of my small living room, with dual sinks, and checkered tile flooring. It was such a lovely bathroom. I looked around at his enormous shower, and saw there was an actual marble bench inside, with multiple small water jets aligned on the wall. My eyes then widened at the huge showerhead in the center of the ceiling that would definitely get the job done by itself.

Who knew that there were so many options for something as basic as cleaning your body? All I'd ever seen was one showerhead, while living at home, and a communal shower at our rented house. But this was on a whole other level. Well good for him. I guess being a professor really did pay well.

Maybe I should have majored in education, instead of science and English. I emptied my bladder and washed my face, and saw a spare toothbrush he'd set on the counter for me, next to his. It was white and purple, and still in the plastic, and I smiled.

I brushed my teeth, and realized that I was practically naked. He must have undressed me last night, because I stood in front of the mirror in only my underwear. I walked back out of the bathroom, to see him still sleeping soundly. I then grabbed my purse, found my dress, and headed out of the room.

I walked down the long hall, passing many doors, then went down the stairs, and after two wrong turns, found the kitchen. It was a massive kitchen, with dual ovens, and a huge range stove. I loved that there was color in the kitchen, and not the typical stainless steel appliances. The cabinets were black with red handles, made with a shiny wood that I wasn't familiar with. But it had an odd antique look to it, and I liked it.

I walked to the back door, and looked out

the curtain. It was such a sunny day. I turned the knob, opening the door, and the alarm suddenly went off. The noise was so loud that I had to cover my ears. I quickly slammed the door closed, and began to pace the kitchen, with my ears covered.

I just didn't know what to do, so I closed my eyes, and tried to zone the deafening sounds out.

The alarm was suddenly shut off, but the sound still rang in my ears, as I held my hands to my ears in a panic. I felt two hands grab my wrists and I screamed. "Baby, it's okay, it's me," he murmured. I opened my eyes to see Thomas standing before me, concern etched all over his face.

"I'm so sorry. I just wanted to step outside, and smell the fresh air," I cried, as he held me closely, as he kissed my head repeatedly, while rubbing my back. I hugged him tightly, needing to feel him close to me, his nearness somehow calmed me

"It's okay. You didn't know, baby," he soothed. He pulled back to look at me, and I knew he could see the light tears that ran down my face. "Hey, no crying. It's okay, you did nothing wrong." I wanted to believe him, but with the alarm sounding, it had turned me into a tense ball of energy, and I knew he could sense it.

"Hey, the code is 3093, alright?" He murmured, looking into my eyes. He looked like he was still half asleep. His hair was tussled and his eyes a little glossy, but he looked so cute. I always wondered how he'd look in the morning, after a night of passion.

He was always clean, fresh, and dressed so fine during his classes. But as I looked at him now, I liked this look better. I tried not to read into the fact that he'd just given me his alarm code. It wasn't as if I would actually need to use it, I honestly didn't think he'd want to see me again after today. My head was clouded with doubt, because I wasn't sure if I could trust him, yet. I still didn't know the man, I only knew the professor.

Things couldn't become too serious between us, with our given history. Not to mention that many women wanted him, for themselves. He was sexy as hell, well groomed, well read, and he was a professor for Christ sake. He lived comfortably and he was amazing in bed, so what would he want with me? I was just me, and I just would not compete for any man's attention.

"I'm sorry again, Thomas. That had to be an alarming way to be woken up," I muttered.

"It was, but it's okay," he slowly kissed my lips, before he wiped my tear-stained cheeks and kissed them. "You didn't eat last night, so I figured I'd cook you breakfast," he went and pulled out bacon, a carton of eggs, coffee, and coffee filters.

"You know I *was* tired, someone wore me out last night," I smiled.

"Hmm. I know the feeling, be right back," he smirked, before he left the kitchen and went down the hall. To what I assumed was another bathroom, because I heard the water running. When he returned, he actually looked refreshed. He came over and kissed me again and I could taste the minty mouthwash, as I kissed him back. *I could get used to his kisses.*

"You know, professor, we could have stayed at the hotel and had their free breakfast," I murmured.

"I know. But I wanted you to see my house

and I wanted to cook for you," he explained.

"I see. Well, I have to get my car and meet my best friend before her flight today. What time is it?" I asked, nervous that it was later than it looked outside.

"It's only nine, you have time, baby."

"Not much. Where are we?" I asked, as he released me. He then went and pulled out an omelet pan, and a small bowl for the eggs. I went and sat on one of the bar stools in front of his kitchen island.

"Home, my home," he said, with a hint of anxiety in his voice.

"I know that much, I meant what area do you live in? How far are we from the hotel?"

"Maybe around twenty miles, I live in Lutherville," he glanced over at me, as my mouth fell open in utter shock.

"You live in, Lutherville?" I asked, bemused.

"Yes, why are you so shocked about that baby?" He asked, perplexed.

"I live here… I mean, I just moved to this area."

"So we're neighbors, huh? What an

interesting coincidence, are you following me, Miss Moore?" he teased, while smiling at me.

"I don't follow *anyone*. I think it's rude and creepy," I snapped.

"Sounds like you have experience in that area," he glanced back at me as he pulled out the eggs. If he only knew how much experience I *did* have in that area.

"Sorry, I didn't mean to snap at you," I exhaled, completely ignoring his silent question for more information as he stared at me. So, I changed the subject. "So, you've lived here long?" I asked, and noticed that he'd turned from filling the coffee maker, and stared at me, totally catching my topic change.

"Maybe five years now, and counting," he uttered, looking perplexed at me having silent deliberations. The last thing I wanted to do, was to tell him that I had a stalker, while attending the university. That was something I didn't want to tell anyone else about, since it was *so* hard for my friends to believe it. But ever since I had moved, I hadn't seen the strange man again, or felt his presence. I took that as a good sign and a chance at a fresh start.

Life was moving along for me, and not in a repetitive circle, like it was while in school. In only a matter of days of graduating college; I'd moved, slept with my Professor, and was about to start a new job. There has been so many changes since I left that area, and I found it to be really amazing, what a nice change of scenery could do for one's life.

Chapter 13

"So you drive twenty miles for work? Is that normal?"

"It is if you like your privacy, and also if you don't want random students popping up on your door, asking you for *"private"* tutoring lessons," he chuckled.

"Wow, that's insane and creepy. You are a desired man, Professor. That alone is an amazing accomplishment all in itself," I then turned and started to walk away from the kitchen, but he came and gently grabbed my arm.

"Where are you going?" He asked, almost panicked, as if he was staring through me *and* my insecurities. I exhaled, and decided to lie.

"I just wanted to take a shower. I don't have much time to get to my car, and I don't want to miss my friend, she's leaving me soon," I said, rambling on.

"You won't miss her, I promise you. You go shower, and I'll cook, okay?"

"Okay," I repeated, and headed off to

submerge myself under his shower. It was such an amazing shower and I took my time washing every inch of body, as I thought about things.

Everything from the last twenty-four hours rushed back to my brain at once, and I actually felt sick, with myself. I had sex with my professor, unprotected sex at that. I stayed the night in house, in an orgasmic coma for most of the night. Now I was here, showering in his massive bathroom, while he cooked me breakfast. *Who was I, and how the hell did I get here?*

I dried off and slipped on my dress, minus my black thong that had somehow disappeared while I was in the shower. *Just great!* I reminded myself to stop somewhere, and pick up some fresh panties, once I got my car from the hotel. Now I was ready to go. I headed back to the kitchen and saw that he had jelly, butter, sugar and creamer laid out nicely, with hot coffee on the table as well. But I didn't really have an appetite anymore. I needed to get to the pharmacy and get the Plan B pill, before I found myself in limbo.

I sat at his bar, as he maneuvered around his

kitchen. As much as I tried not to have a mental breakdown, I felt as if it was happening anyway, while I stared into space.

"What is it, baby, what's wrong?" He asked, as he set a plate of bacon, eggs and toasted English muffin in front me. "Jessica?"

"I'm fine. Just bracing myself." I took a slow sip of coffee and closed my eyes, savoring the taste and warmth of it.

"Bracing yourself, for what?" he asked, as he sat across from me, as he picked up his coffee and took a sip. He looked very worried as he sat across from me, with only pajama bottoms on.

"Well, I am bracing myself about the pill I have to take today…to ensure that you haven't impregnated me," I stated, with no emotion whatsoever. A moment later I peeked up at him and I could tell he was upset. I knew his angry face all too well from last week in class, as he glared at me then… and right now.

"You *don't* have to take that, Jessica," he gritted out.

"What?"

"Why can't we see what happens, is that so

bad?" He spat at me. *Whoa Professor!!*

"Thomas, I-I'm sorry, but I need to get going. Thanks for breakfast, and everything." I said warily, before standing and grabbing my purse, and quickly heading for the front door.

"Jessica, wait," he yelled, as he made his way to me. "What is it, tell me?" He asked, as our eyes locked.

"It's just, I feel as if I'm... I'm—"

"You're not, baby. Neither of us did anything wrong by being together, I promise," he explained and I gave him a tight smile.

"I want to believe you, but I don't think I can."

"Why not?" He asked, as he ran his fingers through my hair and I exhaled.

"I enjoyed myself...I enjoyed you, too much, I think," I blushed, as he chuckled.

"I enjoyed you too, baby, way too much," he winked, pulling me closer to him.

"Really? I'm not very experienced."

"You were amazing, Jessica, and I don't want *this* to end," he stated, as I swallowed rather loudly.

"I can tell, but we can't have a baby. I will

get on the shot or something, if you want to see me again, on a more regular basis."

"I do want to see you again, every day if you let me," he smiled as I tilted my head at him.

"Well, wouldn't that just be... dandy?" I teased.

"Come on and eat your breakfast, baby," he kissed my lips and took my hand into his, as we walked back to his kitchen. "Please stop worrying Jess, one thing at a time. Let's eat and then I will take you back to the hotel in time for your lunch date, okay?"

"Okay." The smile that spread across his face, lit up the entire room. I stepped forward and kissed his lips and he immediately responded, deepening the kiss. He then picked me up and carried me over to his kitchen island, while palming my bare ass. He groaned into our kiss at the same time he squeezed both my ass cheeks, as he pressed himself against me. I wanted him to take me again, right here, on the island. But he didn't. He pulled away from the kiss and just sat me down on a stool, so I could finish eating my breakfast.

"Here, baby, let me get you a hot cup of

coffee," he said, as he picked up my cup.

"No underwear, huh?" He smirked. "Only in my house, Jessica."

"Well, the thin piece of fabric that I call *my underwear* seemed to have disappeared on me, and I have not a clue where it might be." I tapped my chin as we looked at each other, before we both started laughing, hysterically. As he poured me a fresh cup of coffee, I found my eyes admiring his back. He has such a beautiful body and I wanted to bite him and lick him all over, and I was sure that I wasn't the only one. *Stop it, Jess!*

"If you keep eying me like that, I will make sure you miss your impending lunch date," he stated, while his back was turned to me.

"I was just wondering if all your dates get this kind of treatment." I asked, as he poured me a fresh cup.

"I am far too busy to date around."

"You seem to have a lot of time for little 'ole me," I teased.

"You're special," he immediately replied and I gasped.

"Am I?" I asked, reading into his tone and

instant reply to my statement. While secretly wondering if I was special to him.

"Very special," he firmly stated, as he sat a hot cup of coffee in front of me and kissed my head.

"Special huh?" I mocked him, as he turned to face me. I watched in silence as he took a few quick bites of his food and then went upstairs, without saying a word. *Why would I be special to him?* I took a piece of bacon and ate it, while I checked my phone. I had a few missed calls and texts, all from Sherry. I quickly glanced at her texts.

Jess, where the hell r u? 9:56pm

Where did you go? I am outside. 10:06pm

I'm up packing, are we still meeting before my flight? 8:47am

I took a deep breath and then hit speed dial number two. "Hey, Jess, where the hell are you?" She yelled in the phone. I knew I was on her speakerphone from the echo in the background, as she rumbled around packing.

"You wouldn't believe me if I told you. Are we still on for lunch?" I replied.

"Yes, where should we meet?"

"I can meet you at the Marriot, or at our spot near campus?" I offered.

"Our spot would be good. There is nothing like a good chicken and cheese sub. One last hoorah, before I head away for a while. So where are you?" She pressed.

"Can we talk about it later, please?" I whispered.

"Are you alright?" I could hear the concern in her voice.

"I'm fine. See you at our spot at two?" I asked her, needing to get her off the phone, before she started her inquisition.

"Two it is, see you later."

"Okay, see you soon." I hung up and took a few forkfuls of eggs, and another piece of bacon. This was really good, even though it was cold now. I walked over to the back door, looking at the huge backyard. I wanted to see more of it, but I hesitated to open the door. I knew he'd turned the alarm off earlier, but I wondered if it would sound again. I grabbed the knob and began to turn it slowly.

"It's okay, baby, you can open it now," he murmured softly, as I then turned to see him walking towards me. He'd changed into black jeans and a grey V-neck sweater and he looked damned good. The closer he got to me, his scent began to overpower me. This man was a true danger to my senses.

"You look nice," I said as I continued to eye fuck him.

"You look beautiful," he whispered close to my mouth. He then tugged on my bottom lip with his teeth, inciting a soft moan from me. He buried his hand into my hair and gently tugged my head to the side and trailed his mouth up my neck, before planting a kiss near my ear, causing me to mewl.

"Hmm... if you keep making those sexy ass sounds baby, you really won't make it on time," he kissed my lips as he squeezed my ass. *Yes, please!* I needed to distract myself before I called Sherry myself and cancelled.

"Can we stop by my house, so I can change?"

"As long as we're on the road by noon, we should be fine."

"Okay, I will be quick, I promise," I said, he nodded and grabbed my hand.

"Come on, let me show you the yard," he opened the door and we stepped out into the yard. The yard was so big, I assumed it was at least two acres. The grass was trimmed perfectly and I could imagine a dog having a blast with so much space. There were gorgeous trees aligning the yard, and sent a nice subtle breeze our way. I took a few deeps breaths of the fresh air and found myself becoming jealous, that he lived in such a beautiful home.

"This place is amazing. The yard is huge and the air quality seems purified," I beamed at him.

"I'm very glad you like it baby, I was worried you wouldn't," he murmured, as we walked around the yard, holding hands. I turned to him and he was looking at me, anxiously.

"Why would you be worried if I liked your house or not?" I asked bemused, as he looked away from me.

"What man do you know, wouldn't appreciate a woman's opinion, especially on matters as such?" He waved his hand towards the house.

"I see your point. So, why do you have so

much space? I mean, why such a huge house for a single man?"

"I don't plan to be single for long, Jessica. I do want to settle down and have a family one day, very soon."

"Well, whoever she is will be very lucky to have you," I muttered, trying not show my disappointment on his future plans, that wouldn't involve me. With all that he has to offer, any woman would be honored to be his. I was sure he would have the life he longs for, it was just too bad that it wouldn't be with me. I already knew what this was, between us, and what it wasn't. To put it simply; I knew that I didn't qualify for the professor's heart.

"I hope you have all that you want in life, Thomas," I sighed, and he cupped the sides of my face.

"Do you meant that?" He muttered, looking deeply into my eyes, as I nodded.

"Yes, what's so strange about what I said?" I asked.

"I don't want to answer that," he whispered, as if he was choked with an unnamed emotion.

"Is there really anything to be said?" I

replied.

"Plenty," he replied.

"I'll say," I giggled

"What's so funny?" He asked.

"Nothing," I grinned and he grinned back at me.

"You can tell me anything, Jessica."

"I was just thinking that if we were together, like *together,* I would definitely live here. We would be living here together, and taking advantage of this massive yard. I would have cooked *you* breakfast this morning and to think, we could possibly be expecting a baby right now," he just stared at me and his face was emotionless and I flushed. "I…I'm sorry for even telling you that, it sounds so juvenile. It just crossed my mind, and I didn't want to lie about what I was thinking," I rambled on, as he squeezed my hand tighter.

"Can you give me that, Jessica?" He asked, and I gaped at him. As I look into his face, I could immediately tell that he was dead serious. A long moment of silence passed and I knew he could see the panic on my face, as he began to speak. "I want that life with you, Jessica," he stated, with such determination that I blinked at him a few times. *What??*

"Professor, we hardly know each other," I panicked.

"I think we do know each other, but we can take our time and get to know each other better," he grinned and shrugged, looking so intensely at me, while awaiting my response. I didn't think I even qualified for his future, but he's telling me that I did and it was freaking me out. *He wanted more.* If I was honest with myself, I wanted more too, but at a much slower pace.

"Um, can we talk about this another time? I...ugh, I need to meet Sherry," I muttered. I peeked up at him and he looked very upset.

"Okay fine, let's go," he snapped, and gently pulled me towards his truck. As we headed towards my house it dawned on me that I never told him where I lived. But now we were right outside my new building without me telling him a thing. I hopped out and went inside, leaving him in the truck to get himself together. I wasn't sure I wanted him in my house now, especially after what just happened. *I needed to process things and fast.*

It took me all of twenty minutes to freshen up once inside my house. I hurried and changed into a dress and some flats, put on some fresh underwear and a little makeup, and headed back outside.

I pulled opened his passenger door and he just looked over at me. I was hoping that he wasn't still upset with me, and his smile told me that he wasn't. The man couldn't even stay mad at me, he didn't allow his anger to consume him at all. *Oh no, this was bad.* "You're so fucking beautiful, Jessica," he growled, sending a shiver down my spine.

"Thank you," I replied and climbed into his truck. "I'm sorry I took so long."

"You were only gone for twenty minutes, that was great timing," he smiled and I smiled back. We sat in silence for most of the ride back to the Marriott, and it was deafening. I just didn't know what to say to him, and I still didn't know if I wanted things to progress with us in the way he wanted. I was still getting over the fact that I'd slept with my professor, and it didn't make matters any easier knowing that it was the best sex of my life.

I knew underneath it all, that he was still upset. Which told me so much more that I even knew, about the way he feels about me. This whole time I always thought he wasn't interested me, but I was wrong. He must have been fighting his attraction to me, just like I was to him. Oh God, and now I just slept with him. I needed to seriously digest all this, and I needed to get away from him to do that. I knew now that his feelings must run really deep, if he was already proposing a life with me. A life any woman would want with a man like him, but he was thinking too far ahead, w*ay too far ahead.*

Chapter 14

"You did WHAT??" Sherry screeched at me, making heads turn towards us in the hoagie shop, as my cheeks flamed in utter embarrassment. I anxiously glanced around and then lowered my head, as she continued her rant.

"Hold on. Wait a damned minute, *Jessica*." She spat my name out, as if it were a poisonous weapon.

"Sherry, please—"

"I've been waiting for almost four years, *four years,* for you to live a little, and fuck some random guy. Now, when my flight leaves in," she looked at her watch, then back up at me, "Three hours and seventeen minutes...You're telling me you've not only been fucking some guy all night, but it just so happens to be the man that ninety percent of the population in this area *wants*?" She growled at me. *Omg!*

"Yes, and please calm down. Just hearing you say all that makes me feel sick," I muttered. She fell silent and just glared at me, as if she couldn't find the words to speak in that moment. All she did was pick up the other half of her chicken and cheese sub and take a big bite, while shaking her head at me and giggling.

"Sher, I didn't mean for it happen, it just kind of did. I guess I was at the right place at the right time, and a little tipsy," I explained.

"There is no such thing, Jess. Your timing was perfect, because it was *supposed* to be perfect. Tell me; how did you snag this man, Jess. I have to know?" She asked incredulously, while she chewed her food gazing at me.

"I don't even know the answer to that myself, Sherry, I swear. I could barely talk around him, because I was so nervous. The things he would say to me, had my mind constantly spinning and I couldn't think straight," I admitted, to not only her, but to myself as well. How is it that, Thomas, makes me nervous and scatters my brain, but not Professor Brennan?

"What was he saying to you?" She inquired, with an arched brow.

"He was pleasant, attentive, and very interested in spending time with me. Which is normal when getting to know someone better, right?" She nodded.

"Riiiiight, and…" she sung.

"But then he would say something so out of the blue, and it would startle me completely."

"Like what, Jess? I'm drooling here, so spill?" She urged, eyes widening.

"I won't go into too much detail, but he definitely wants more of this *thing* with me and him. He also asked me if I would want to have his baby. Not now of course, but maybe later on."

"What the *fuck!*" She screeched, causing heads to turn into our direction again as I flushed. In that instance, I just wanted to crawl under the table and put up a tent and roast marshmallows while singing old songs by The Monkeys. Due to my overly expressive best friend.

Sherry was always one to *love* a good story. She didn't like spreading gossip, but she loved to listen to others talk. She was almost like a spy. Whoever had the juice…she would always be at the right place and time to hear them talk about it. She had shared some stories with me most nights, while we lived at the house, and they were always good. Whether it was about someone's sporadic hookup, breakup or about one of our roommate's crazy dating lives.

There seemed to always be someone who did something totally stupid. Things like cheating, or even as reckless as having unprotected sex, which sometimes led to an infection, or possible pregnancy that someone tried their best to hide. They weren't good at keeping things from Sherry, she always found out and delivered the goods.

She was so good, that she even had Intel on Professor Brennan's fan club. But not today. Today I was the one with the story, and she couldn't contain her excitement not one bit. Her best friend, known as the wallflower of the house, finally had something to share with her. Even though it was embarrassing, it was also exciting. "Jessica, he more than likes you. He wants to marry you," she grinned. *What? The? Hell??*

"Oh please, don't be ridiculous, Sherry. We don't even know each other well enough, to even go there," I scoffed.

"So, you're telling me that you don't want *more* of what he has to offer?" She asked, knowing the answer already. But I had to be strong now and not show weakness, even if he came in a delectable package that I wanted all to myself, one day.

Truth was; I wasn't some young naïve girl desperate to be in league with her professor, he has a fan club for that kind of thing. I was just a college graduate, who was still finding her way. I had to be careful not to become too distracted with anyone, or anything. "Jess, answer the question."

"Okay, don't get me wrong, Sher. I would love all he has to offer, on a nightly basis," I smirked, and she instantly raised her hand in the air for a "high five" as she screeched. I smacked her hand and giggled at my crazy friend. Who is going to get us kicked out of the hoagie shop if she doesn't calm the hell down.

"That's my girl," she boasted.

"But, I don't know if it would work? You know…the ex-teacher, ex-student thing kind of bothers me," I admitted.

"Well, all that doesn't matter now. You both

are consenting adults and free to do as you please," she stated proudly.

"Yeah, that's what he said," I sighed.

"Wait a minute... wait a *damn* minute. He actually said that to you?" I looked at her to see her griping the edges of the table tightly as she pierced me with her stare. She looked at me almost as if she saw President Obama standing behind me. She was in shock, while frantically waiting for me for to respond.

"Yes, he really did say that to me."

"Oh my," she uttered and sat back in her chair, suddenly deep in thought.

"Sher, why are you so—"

"That means he wanted you when you were his student, Jess. He actually wanted you for all those years, and the fucker actually waited for you. Ohmygod, this is just too much for me to handle, I may have a meltdown. Fuck, you are one lucky *bitch*," she spat and exhaled.

"Why am I deemed lucky just because he wants *me?* He's a man who likes a woman, what's so grand about that?" I mocked.

"I'll tell you what's so grand about it *best-friend*. It's because *you* are that woman, and *he* is that man. If he waited for you... than this *thing* between the two of you, is much more than just some random fling to him. Please Jess, for love of God, start reading in between the lines. I know you don't have much experience with men, but trust me when I tell you. This man really likes you, and I think you should see where it leads," she stated, proudly.

"He says he doesn't date much at all and that he doesn't take what's offered to him from his fan club. He says that he has to want it too... and what he wants is me," she blinked a few times at me, as I quickly took a bite of my steak and cheese sub.

"Jessica, Jessica, Jessica. You have to listen to me babe, this is a good thing happening for you. You are both grownups and what really matters is that there was no ill-will done, while you were his student. Was there?" I shook my head, and took a sip of my ginger ale.

"None whatsoever," I said.

"Good, and you can say that with pride and in truth. You have got to give him a chance to know you, and be with you."

"I really hadn't plan on dating anyone, not

for a while at least."

"Plans can change," she winked.

"The man scrambles my brain completely, with his presence, his touch and his words. So I need to keep my distance from him for now, until I figure out what it is I want, or don't want for that matter."

"Why? No, you don't need any more time to do that. He may move, or disappear, or meet someone else, and then what?"

"I need to focus on getting my life and career started, Sher. This *thing* between us, I mean, where could it go?" I still had my doubts about him and us, but I couldn't deny the curiosity that consumed my mind as we talked.

"News flash girl. Your life has already started, and I would trade places with you in a second," she stated, and snapped her finger with a sharp snap. I couldn't stop myself from laughing at her.

"My best friend is *crazy*."

"Certified!" She boasted and I laughed again. "So, don't hold out on me...how was the sex?" She leaned in to hear the juice, as I took a deep breath.

"So good that I plead the fifth, sixth, seventh and eight…" I smirked, and she nodded.

"I'm not surprised, I always knew he would be an amazing fuck. My God, Jess, this is the best juice I've had in my entire college career," she sighed, and I shook my head at her. "It's such a shame it had to happen when I'm leaving, but I *will* be needing weekly updates," she scowled at me.

"I'm sure you will. You're the only person I can talk to about this, and now you're leaving me." I pursed my lips at her.

"I'll be in Jersey, but I will come back in a few months to see you. Until then, we have the phone and text messages," she reminded me.

"Yes we do."

"We'll have a girl's weekend when I come back in a few months, and if I can swing it earlier than that, I will," she smiled. Sherry had to go take care of her mother, who had grown ill over the last few weeks. She had wanted to give herself some time to look for a good job here, but now that her mother was ill, she was going back home to live and care for her.

"I'm going to miss you so much, but you

won't be too far. I can always catch a bus or drive up," I smiled.

"You sure can, that would be great and you can bring the professor with you," she smirked. "Look, if things don't work out with him, then it doesn't. But promise me that you'll give yourself the chance to see if it could? Jess, there is nothing like being wanted by someone who is willing to put his desires aside for the benefit of your future," she stated.

"His future would have been at stake too, but yes, he did a good job of taming his feelings for me while we were in that situation. I really didn't have a clue that he even, liked me."

"This is just so amazing and I am happy for you, Jess. So what's next for you after you leave me?" She asked, as I swallowed hard.

"Well, I need to head to the pharmacy and pick up the morning after pill, before I wind up carrying his child a month from now," I explained, and watched as the color drained from Sherry's face. She was in no way prepared to hear that, and a part of me instantly regretted telling her how irresponsible we'd been last night. But I had to send her off with something that would not only occupy some of her flight, but the entire flight back home.

After we hugged and kissed, she'd left still in a state of shock, and I left the hoagie shop and headed towards my apartment. I didn't want to get the pill in this area, so my plan was to wait until I got near my house, to pick it up. The entire way I was deep in thought, as I tried to digest all that had happened recently, in my ordinarily boring life.

Chapter 15

When he climbed into his bed that night, he couldn't believe his eyes. There she was, Jessica Moore, in his bed sound asleep. He felt as if his life had become surreal as he gazed at her beautiful skin and parted lips, wondering if she was dreaming about him. Once he pulled her body close to his, and she snuggled closer to him of her own accord, he was in pure bliss.

To be able to touch her so intimately, made him feel as if he was the luckiest man in the world. As they slept, he kept his arm locked around her and his nose buried in her hair. He was in heaven. He hadn't slept so deeply in years, and he knew it was because she was right where he wanted her to be. In his arms.

After the first kiss, the first touch and the first taste of her, he couldn't control his urge to devour her repeatedly. But he knew he had too, because this all was new for her and he had to remember that. He didn't want to come on too strong or take any chances of ruining his new relationship with her.

Whether she knew it or not, this was not some casual fling to him. This was more. This was definite... Jessica Moore was his future. With their relationship *finally* taking a new turn, this had made him delirious happy. Being around her always made him happy, but now he could touch her, feel her and see her in ways he never could before. Which excited him to no end, but it was her response to him that excited him most. She wanted him... and he knew it.

No matter how hard she tries to fight it, he won't let her give up on them, especially when they'd just made it out of uncharted territory. It was the morning after and in his eyes, things were going as great as could be expected, between them. Until he scared her with talk of the future, a little too soon.

As they headed back into town, they rode in silence the entire way, and he didn't like it. He knew he needed to stay calm, regardless of her deafening silence. So in the hopes of not arguing with her, he'd kept quiet, while his own thoughts consumed him. He just didn't understand what he did wrong. Why wasn't she excited to hear the things he was proposing to her?

He knew that if he had asked anyone else to have his child and be with him in every way, they would jump at the chance. But the one he actually wanted that with, just looked back at him in disgust, and that was a hard pill for him to take.

***

Professor Brennan found himself still in deep thought, as he sipped more wine while staring at the photo framed on his desk. It was a photo of Jessica he'd managed to get from a group photo taken of his class, where he'd cropped her out and framed the photo, which lived on his desk in his home office.

He was alone in his house, and he felt his mind spinning with unanswered questions. He just didn't understand what he did wrong? Women normally ate out of the palm of his hand, without him even trying. He kept wondering why Jessica wouldn't allow herself to need him, when she was all alone in a new town?

If it were anyone else, he would have turned

the other way by now, but it wasn't anyone else. It was her. He knew he didn't want anyone else, even before they slept together last night. But since he's had a taste of her, he knew that there was no going back, not now or ever.

He wanted *her*, and the idea of her not wanting him made him depressed, and the thought of another man having her made him sick. After another hour of mental deliberations, he stood and downed the rest of *her* favorite wine, before he headed up the stairs to the second floor of his home.

He went inside one of his guest-rooms and headed into the closet, and pulled out a black duffle bag. Before heading into his master bedroom, with that same bag. Once inside his bedroom, he'd set the bag down near the edge of his bed, and just looked at the side of the bed where she'd slept only a few hours ago. He reached for her pillow and clutched it close to him, with both hands.

Before he buried his nose in it, desperately needing to smell her intoxicating scent. He hadn't had unprotected sex since he was a teenager, and to have that experience again, with

Jessica, just furthered his infatuation with her. As his eyes closed, he thought back to the way she screamed his name, as her plush walls milked him repeatedly. How she dug her nails into his back and shoulders, sending pain coursing throughout his body, igniting him to pound into her even harder... and she fucking loved it.

It was the best sex of his life, and he had no doubt that he would do anything to have her be with him, no matter what that entailed. His mind was made up and he began to strip off his clothes from earlier. He quickly showered and brushed his teeth, to devoid himself of any scents or cologne that she would now recognize.

Then he unzipped the black duffle bag. He removed a pair of black jeans, a black hoodie, and a grey t-shirt and quickly dressed. Then he grabbed his phone and pressed a few buttons rather quickly, before tossing it on the bed. Then he dug back inside the duffle bag and pulled out a dark blue cap, with **NY** threaded in white letters. He placed the cap onto his head as his phone began chirping repeatedly.

The sound of his phone chirping had his

mind racing, as he stared at it for a few moments. The sound was a special tone, a tone that was programed for one purpose. It alerted him to Jessica's location, from the tracker placed on her car. As he checked his phone, he saw that she was already back in town. He googled the address she was located at, and saw that she was at the drug store. The thought of why she was there, immediately filled him with dread.

He didn't want her to kill his semen that was deep inside of her tight little cunt. He wanted it to do the job it was made to do, which was to fertilize *her* eggs. He knew that both pills needed to be taken for it to work, with a twelve-hour interval between each pill, which made his plans for tonight to immediately change.

Watching her wouldn't be as effective for tonight, he needed to do more. He needed more time with her so he can convince her to be with him, in every way that he needed her to be. He needed to get her to need him.

But first, he needed to confirm if she'd taken the first pill, and then he needed to ensure that she didn't take the second one. He was sure she would have had taken the first already, knowing her. But he'd be damned if she was going to take that second pill, he just needed to find a way to distract her… and he already had an idea of how.

Chapter 16

It was such a relaxing drive home, letting my windows down and enjoying the warm salty breeze sifting through my hair. I was only five minutes away from my destination, and my thoughts drifted back to Thomas. All this time I thought I wouldn't see him again, and within the last twenty-fours, so much had changed between us.

We went on a date, had mind-blowing sex and it all ended with a sleep-over at his place. I just couldn't believe it, it didn't make any sense to me at all how any of this happened. Not to mention that we are both now living in the same area. The night of jazz, the sex and his proposal of wanting to be with me, had me thinking non-stop. I was truly living in the twilight zone.

I pulled up to the drug store and sat inside my car for what seemed like hours, before I'd gotten out and headed inside the store. I went straight to the pharmacy, and after a brief chat with the pharmacist, I was now leaving with two little pink pills and a mild migraine.

I took one of the pink pills immediately, with my bottle of water I had in my car, and began the rest of my journey home. When I arrived home, I parked my car and went inside.

My building was small and quaint and only had three floors, and there were four apartments on each floor. It seemed pretty quiet around here from what I could already tell, and I loved that. Once inside my small apartment, I dropped my bag on the counter and grabbed a water from my refrigerator.

I sat on my couch to re-read the instructions of the morning after pill, in more detail. I found myself giggling at the disclaimer, which basically stated that there was a one percent chance it wouldn't work. Most pharmaceutical companies were scared of that one hundred percent guarantee, and I get it.

They didn't want to take the heat, if their product didn't work, which would result in many lawsuits for them. I heard my phone chime and I hopped up and grabbed it out of my purse, and saw that I had a text from Thomas.

"Please tell me that you're alright?" -PB

I hadn't planned on talking to him until I

knew what to say, but what the hell. I might as well talk to him now, since he's reached out. I couldn't just leave him hanging. I honestly didn't expect to even still be on his mind, but I wasn't mad that I was. He was so caring and attentive, and those were qualities that I really liked about him.

"Yes, I am okay. How are you?" -JM

"Good. Thinking about you, I want to see you again." –PB

"I want to see you, too. –JM

"Which day would be good for you?" –JM

"Whichever day is good for me. –PB

"Have you taken that pill?" -PB

"Yes, I took it twenty minutes ago. I'm due to take the other in exactly twelve hours, so I've set my alarm to get up early. –JM

"How early are we talking?" -PB

"Eight o'clock early, why?"-JM

"Can see each other for dinner tomorrow night?" -PB

"Okay, an early dinner sounds good. I do have a new job to start on Monday." -JM

"I haven't forgotten. I look forward to

seeing you tomorrow evening, sleep well, baby." -PB

"Goodnight, Professor ;)" -JM

I set my phone down and took a very long shower, washing my hair and cleaning my skin a few times more than necessary. I was still in a funk over having to take these pills, while wondering what was happening inside of my body right now. I finally made it out of the shower and made a toasted peanut butter and jelly sandwich, before climbing into bed with a glass of milk and started watching television.

After I'd eaten, I closed my blinds and got back into bed. I had drifted off to sleep rather quickly, while dreaming of a certain professor.

***

I groaned while awakening to the light that was shining throughout my bedroom. A light so bright, that it had literally made it impossible for me to continue sleeping. I knew my blinds were thin, but they should have been able to shield some of that blinding light. I groaned again and covered my head with my pillow, but the light still seeped through somehow.

I cracked my eyes open and looked over towards the window, to see that my blinds were up and open. *What the hell?* I sat up, slowly, while staring at the open blinds. Knowing for a fact that I had closed them before bed last night.

My eyes slowly roamed around my room, as I started to be consumed with doubt. I could sense that something was wrong here, something was out of order. I felt uneasy and very disturbed about the blinds being open. But maybe it was nothing, maybe I opened them in the middle of the night. *Yep, I will go with that before I drove myself crazy.*

These feelings of paranoia were still new to me, but since moving, I am trying not to let them overwhelm me anymore. I raised my hands high in the air, as if I was trying to touch the ceiling, from my bed. I always stretched that way, every single morning. After a few seconds, I flung my arms back down on the bed, and something pricked me on the hand.

"Oww," I squeaked, as I grabbed my other hand, and saw a red bruise forming and it hurt like hell.

I glanced over my bed, looking for what

poked me. My mouth fell open, as I slowly picked up a single white rose with thorns lying on my adjacent pillow, while the color drained from my face. I quickly looked around my room again as panic seized me, I knew that someone had to have been in here. *What the fuck!!*

I hopped up and grabbed my cell phone, as I awkwardly put on my pants. I quickly dialed the police, as I rummaged my nightstand looking for my mace. Once I found it, I slowly walked towards my bedroom door, with my phone pressed to my ear.

"Nine-one-one… what is your emergency?" A female operator answered.

"Hello, yes I need some help. Someone was in my apartment while I was sleeping last night, please, I'm scared," I rambled on, slowly peeking out of my bedroom door. I was scared to death, and panicked. *Was someone still in here?*

"Are you sure, ma'am?" The operator asked me.

"I am positive. Hurry, I don't know if they're still here. Can you send someone, please?" I cried.

"Okay, we will be right there ma'am, just try to stay calm. What is your name, and where are you now?" She asked.

"Jessica Moore, and I'm in my bedroom. I was going to search the apartment."

"No, stay inside your bedroom, and lock the door until we get there," she ordered.

"Okay, can you stay on the phone with me, please?" I asked.

"Sure, breathe Jessica, we're on the way," she confirmed. After hearing the police bang on my door, like the four horseman of the apocalypse. The operator confirmed that it was okay to exit my room, and then I ran to my door and let them in. They searched the entire place and found nothing. They took the white rose for evidence, and dusted for fingerprints around my windows and doors. After they took my information, they told me that there wasn't any evidence of a forced entry. Which didn't make me feel *any* better, at all.

They then recommended that I stay with a friend for a few days, until they get back to me. I was so shaken about the whole thing, that I felt sick to my stomach. I didn't know how or why anyone would want to break into my apartment, but I had idea who this may be. *Who in the hell was stalking me? How did this maniac know where I lived? How did he get inside of here?*

I told the police that I had a stalker while in school, but since I never filed a report, it did nothing for my claims on the matter. Nothing at all.

Almost two hours later, they were gone and I was packing a suitcase with no destination in sight.

I just knew I couldn't stay there. I contacted the rental office and informed them of everything. They suggested that they could move me into another apartment, but it wouldn't be for another month or two. They were fully occupied at the moment, and that was not good news for me.

After packing some clothes and a few outfits for work, I headed to my car. I sat there wondering what I should do. I didn't want to worry my parents, or my best friend with this just yet. Because I needed to find a place to stay, and I didn't know where I could go. I didn't have money to live in a hotel, but I could stay there for a few days at least, until I figured something out. I grabbed my phone to google the nearest hotel, when I saw a text from Thomas.

"Making my special chicken for you tonight. I have it marinating now. Can't wait for you to taste it, baby. I miss you." -PB

I stared at his message, as tears began to fall down my face. Why was it that *now* I could cry about all this? Instead of texting him back, I called him and he answered on the second ring.

"I'm so happy you called, baby," he answered.

He sounded so happy and carefree, and I realized that I was the complete opposite. My words were taken from me in that instant, and all I could do was sob harder. I sniffed and whimpered into the phone. "Baby? Jessica, are you crying… what's wrong?" He blurted.

"Everything," I cried. That was all I could muster up to say to him, I felt so lost.

"Where are you right now?" He yelled. I could hear him running down the stairs, his keys jingling into the phone. I swallowed and tried to stop my heaving to talk to him, but it was proving to be difficult.

"In, my, parking lot. In, my, car," I heaved.

"I'm coming. Stay there okay, baby?" I heard him start his ignition and then I heard his tires screeching. I dropped the phone on the floor of my car, and wrapped my arms around my steering wheel, lowering my head onto it and just cried. It was all I could seem to do, until I heard a car screech to an insane halt beside mine. I'd kept my head down because I knew who it was already. As he began knocking on my window, I lifted my head and when we made eye contact, he looked sick with worry.

I unlocked my door, and he opened it and slowly lifted me out the car. I wrapped my arms around his neck and sobbed into his shoulder, as he kissed my head.

I closed my eyes and tightened my hold on him, as he walked me over to his truck, and set me inside the passenger side. I looked up at him and gave a slight smile, and took a deep shaky breath, as he gazed at me in panic. He then wiped my tears with his thumbs, as he held my face in his hands.

"Thomas, I'm being stalked," his eyes

widened, as I heard his sharp intake of air.

"What do you mean, *stalked*?" He demanded.

"It started while I was in school. I felt that I was being followed, but I didn't think much of it. Until I saw the guy myself one day, after leaving the library. I couldn't see him clearly that night, and before I got any closer, he vanished. I saw him again and he pulled me from the street, and saved me from being hit by a truck. He saved my life. Now, someone has broken into my house last night while I was sleeping, and left a rose on the pillow right next to me and-and... I'm freaking out," I cried, the unstoppable tears flowing again, down my face. He grabs my hand, holding it tightly. "I have no place to go, and I need to—"

"You'll move in with me. We will handle this together," he stated.

"Professor, I don't want to impose on you like that," I muttered.

"Baby, I want you there, where I can keep you safe. I can't let anything happen to you. I want you safe. I need you safe, okay?" He pleaded, I knew I needed his help, so I just nodded my head.

"The police will call me in a few days if they get prints or anything. I may have to move from here, I just don't know what—"

"Jessica, stop worrying. You can think about all that later. Let's get your things and go back to my place."

"I have a suit case in my trunk, but I didn't pack much. I was rushing to get out of there."

"Let's go back inside. We'll pack properly so you can have what you want with you. Or we can buy you knew things, whichever you'd prefer," he offered.

"I can't go back in there yet. I need to stop crying first," I sniffed.

"Okay, I'm here, and I will take care of you," he promised, as he placed a soft kiss on my face, both my eyes and my lips.

"Thank you, so much."

"Jess, I'm sorry this happened to you, and I hope they find whoever did this. But don't worry, you don't have to stay here, you have my place now. I'll get your suitcase out of the car and we'll go," I nodded and he went and grabbed my suitcase and drove us to his home, which wasn't that far away. Once there, he took my things to one of his guest-rooms, and I looked over at him, somewhat shocked. "Would you prefer to stay in here, or in my room?" He asked.

"I'll stay in here, I don't want to crowd you too much," I smiled.

"You won't, Jessica, I assure you... but it's your call. My door is always open for you, any time of the day or night, alright?"

"Okay, thank you. You're so sweet, Thomas," he smiled, and kissed my cheek, and set my suitcase down. *The woman who snags this man will be a very lucky lady.*

I started to unpack, while he opened the blinds and cracked the window, in this dimly lit room. He opened the closet door and turned the light on, and was now making sure the bathroom was stocked with the proper necessities.

It was a spacious room decorated in green and blue, the bed was bigger than my own and I couldn't complain. I was just glad he offered to help me, regardless of all of my issues. In some strange way, he calms me... and I liked that. Aside from craziness of things, I was just happy to be here, with him.

"Jessica, I will have some clothes delivered for you by tomorrow, and I'll have your car moved here by night fall. I'm going to make a few calls, and make us some lunch, okay?"

"Okay, I'll take a shower and be right down."

"Take your time baby, and relax. I've got you," he kissed my forehead, and left the room. Instead of overthinking things, I decided the best to do was to finish unpacking. I only had a little bit of clothes with me, and a few toiletries, that I had placed in the bathroom. I turned the shower on and tried to wash away the last few horrific hours, with soap and water.

Chapter 17

He'd walked the five blocks back to his truck that was located on a side street with his cap worn low, and his head down. Once inside his truck, he slammed the door closed and exhaled. The anxiety of what he has been doing to her, was starting to weigh on his conscience and not in a good way. But he pushed his wayward thoughts aside and started his engine and pulled off.

It was early morning, so the sidewalks were bare, and there was very little traffic on the streets. Which he already knew and used to his advantage. For what he had planned to do, he needed to get in and out with minimal chance of being seen. So early morning was the only way, and now he was headed back to his house. To await the urgent phone call that he knew would come in the next hour or so, once she woke up.

Two hours had passed and the call he was waiting for, never came. He began to worry and decided to send her a text message. He needed to make himself present, even if she wasn't thinking about him at that very moment.

So he texted her, letting her know that he was thinking about her and making sure that he was in some way, on her mind. He anxiously began pacing around his kitchen, wondering why she still hadn't called him yet. He then went upstairs to wash his face, and brace himself for her call. Then, a few minutes later, the call he was waiting for, finally came. But to his dismay, it was in no way what he'd expected it to be like.

He anticipated that she would be upset, and maybe a little startled, but she was more than both of those things put together. She was hysterical. She was crying uncontrollably, frightened and hyperventilating when she called him. It seemed as if she was on the verge of having a panic attack. Once he held her in his arms, he kept trying to calm her down, but it wasn't working. The guilt started to weigh on him even more, he felt so cruel for putting her through this. But the pros outweighed the cons of his actions, so he didn't allow himself to feel too bad.

He needed her to see the bigger picture, and

this was the only way he knew how to do that. He just didn't want to waste any more time, and he knew all that he'd done was necessary, to a good extent.

Because now she was exactly where he wanted her to be, where he felt she belonged, all along. She was now staying with him, in his home and in some sick and twisted way, he couldn't be happier.

***

After he'd made a few calls to get her car moved to his home, and to his personal shopper to deliver her a full wardrobe ASAP. He then made his way to the kitchen, to make them some lunch. He'd prepared the table on the patio, since she really liked the yard, and he knew she could use the fresh air.

He set the pitcher of lemonade on the table, along with the plated turkey sandwiches he'd made. He was tossing the salad, when she came outside, and as he looked up, his heart stopped at the sight of her. She had on blue jeans, a white camisole top and some flats. "Hi?" She uttered.

"Hello, I was just, umm...preparing lunch for us," he nervously explained, while he gazed at her. He then took a deep breath. "Jessica, you're so beautiful, baby," she blushed, and walked over to him and gave him a hug. He immediately dropped the utensils on the table, and pulled her closer to him.

With each breath of her, he could feel his erection hardening to the point of popping the teeth of the zipper on his jeans. He needed to calm himself down. "You smell so good, baby. Please, come and eat, I'm sure you're hungry," he stated.

"I am. Thank you for making lunch...this really looks great," she smiled warmly at him.

"You're welcome. I have Greek salad, and turkey clubs for us today," he smiled.

"Where is this chicken you're so excited for me to taste?" She teased.

"That's for dinner. It has to be properly marinated for at least ten hours. Some things are worth the wait, baby," he kissed her hair and leaned in, pulling her chair out as she sat down. He then sat across from her and smiled, knowing that this was the first of many lunches, they would have together.

He smiled as they talked and ate, she didn't want to talk about what happened and he didn't object, because neither did he. He just wanted to be with her, and he couldn't hide his excitement. *Who could blame him?*

***

After an amazing dinner, paired with some amazing wine, I was feeling restless as we sat on the couch, snuggling and watching a film. I had so much to think about, and not enough time to do it. I appreciated Thomas' hospitality and warmth, but I needed to figure out what was going on here. I had so many questions that I couldn't answer to save my life. Being as though my life was obviously at stake here, I needed to figure this out and fast.

"Hey? Are you okay?" He murmured.

"No, I'm thinking about what's happening to me. I just don't understand it, why me?"

"Things happen to everyone, baby. You have to stay calm, and figure out what your next move is," he murmured into my hair, pulling me closer.

"That sounds about right, but I just can't figure out who this stalker is. I mean, this all started back when I was going to the university, but no one believed me," I explained, and could feel him shift, before he kissed my head softly.

"So, you had seen someone back then, you'd said?" He inquired.

"I did, twice. One of those times he actually saved me from getting hit by a truck, when I was drunk one night."

"Did he now? So, he stalked you and cared enough to save you? That doesn't sound right."

"I know, that's what so confusing. Why scare me half to death and then feel the need to save me, so you can continue to scare me? Maybe all this is a sign, maybe I should move back home to Michigan. I don't need some maniac following me, and being able to break into my house whenever he feels like it. I've never had this issue before I moved here for school." Maybe moving back home wasn't a bad idea. My parents would support my decision on that, they'd actually encourage it.

"Maybe it will stop, now that the police are involved?" He offered.

"Maybe, but what if he comes back to my place, or my next place? I hardly have anyone here with me now, and I can't live my life on the edge of insanity. Regardless of my neighbors, my job...and you, I will be alone a lot. That makes me a target for him, and I'm scared, Thomas," I exhaled, as his arms tightened around me, as I lay on his chest.

"Baby, don't worry. You can live with me and I will take you to and from work, I will keep you safe," he stated firmly, I pulled up to look at him, we were face-to-face as he ran his fingers through my hair, his mouth parting as his eyes lowered to my lips.

"Thank you...for everything, but... I didn't graduate college to become your housemate, and for you to become my personal protection detail."

"Protection detail?" He repeated, and looked as to be considering that idea. "I like that and I think that is a great idea, baby. I will hire someone to be with you while you're out; they will make sure you get to where you're going safely, and bring you back home, with me."

"Home with you?" I asked.

"Yes, home with me. I want you here with me, every day," he stated, before leaning forward and placing a lingering kiss onto my lips. "And every night," he muttered, and kissed my lips again and I kissed him back. As his hands found my waist, I began to climb up and straddle him. I poured all of my frustration and anxiety into the kiss. I kissed him as if I needed him to breathe, to live... to love. My hands were in his hair, and his hands were now on my behind, pushing me further onto him. I began grinding against his erection, as we deepened the kiss. *Oh god!*

A few moments later he pulled back from the kiss, and as I opened my eyes they immediately locked with his. His eyes were burning into mine, as he gently cupped one side of my face with his palm. "Oh baby," he uttered, his voice strained and breathless. I then placed my palm over his hand that cupped my face, my eyes never leaving his. I turned toward it and placed a soft kiss onto the inside of his palm, before I turned back to look at him. His face was blank and intense, I couldn't figure out what it was he thinking. He almost looked lost.

"Kiss me," I whispered close to his mouth as my hand tightened in his hair. Then he kissed me, no hold bars kissing. I could feel him trembling beneath me as he held me close. I moaned into the kiss, as did he, as he tugged my bottom lip with his teeth. Then he grabbed my waist, and stood with me as my legs wrapped around his waist. He slowly lowered me down to the floor, as he pulled his lips from mine. I stood there, watching him, as he took off his shirt and then mine.

"Take off your pants, baby. I want you to sit on my face," he muttered, before he took off his pants, as I continued to undress. I was still nervous about all of this, and now I was even more nervous about it all.

"Thomas?" I uttered, as he sat down on the cream colored bear skinned rug before me, in only his white boxer briefs. He leaned his head backwards, arching his neck onto the couch, as I just looked at him. I had never done that before, and me standing here in front of him, *stark naked*, didn't ease my anxiety one bit. I never would have thought I'd be one who could actually say that, I'd sat on my Professor's face, and he sucked me into an orgasm. But the look of hunger in his eyes was so naughty, and very sexy as he gazed at my nakedness. *Oh God!* He then reached out his hand, and I immediately took it as he pulled me towards him.

"Thomas, wait. I've never done that, and I..."

"Don't worry, I will guide you, baby. I just want to submerge myself into your sweetness, while you ride my face," he uttered darkly, as he smiled wickedly at me. *Oh God!*

He then placed both hands around my thighs, while he licked his lips and I smiled at him. I lowered myself onto the couch, one knee at a time, on either side of his face. As he held onto my thighs, guiding me higher up on him. I then leaned forward, placing my hands on the couch in front of me, for leverage.

With a loud groan, he palmed my hips and pushed me all the way down, exactly where he wanted me, and began to suck on my clitoris. All it took was a few shorts moments, before I felt a rush of heat and moisture covering me. As he continued to suckle me, at just the right time, with the perfect amount of pressure. I began subtle movements against his mouth, before he began to thrust his tongue in and out of me.

"Oh, God," I whimpered, as I found myself surrendering to the pleasure. He now held my ass in both his hands, pushing me further into him, and at the rhythm we'd created together. I moaned as I felt his tongue slowly circling my clitoris, and with precision. "Oh, yes," I moaned loudly, as his tongue delved deeper inside me, as one of hands laid flat on my upper back, controlling his tongue thrusts. As I continued to ground my hips onto his face, I could hear him moaning into me, as his mouth worked wonders on me.

"Professor... my God," I breathed, as my inner walls contracted around his tongue, and I felt as if I was going to *die* from pleasure. I continued to ride his face, with no conviction, as my orgasm was vastly approaching. He groaned into me repeatedly as he devoured me, taking me higher than I've ever been before.

When my orgasm hit, he gripped my ass tighter, as my arms and legs became severely weakened, causing me to lose my stance. He sucked on me hard, as I screamed out causing me to fall over even more over his head and onto the couch, as I continued to writhe in pleasure. Before I knew it, he had lifted me from his mouth and seconds later, I was on all fours on the couch.

With a deep growl, he slammed into me, from behind. He moved at his own pace from behind me, as he took my body, moaning and growling with each thrust. I screamed out with each sharp and powerful thrust of his hips, as my body desperately tried to suck him in even more.

"Mine-*thrust*-All-mine-*thrust*," he groaned. "Give it to me baby-*thrust-thrust*-now-*thrust*," he growled, as he continued to pound into me hard, deep, and relentlessly. He smacked my ass, extracting a deep guttural groan from me as he groped me closer to him.

"Oh, God... oh yes," I moaned, as he took my body to pleasures I'd never known before. We both continued to cry out, as he groped my ass and aggressively palmed my breasts, while swearing loudly.

"Fuck Fuck Fuckkkk!" He yelled, as he grabbed a fist full of my hair. Sounds of intense love making covered the house, and probably the block. We were so loud, and completely full of one another. This was animal sex and I loved it, with him. "Come with me, baby... *Jessica,*" he growled.

"Oh yes, harder... fuck me, Thomas," I cried out.

"Oh, Jessica...baby," he breathed, his voice was strained, almost hoarse as his thrusts picked up speed. We came together, each in a burst of splendor as we jerked and shook around each other. *Incredible!* He then pulled me into his arms and kissed my lips and my forehead reverently, as we snuggled closer.

A few minutes later, I found myself dozing off while listening to the steady beating if his heart, as I lay on his chest. As we both were still trying to control our breathing.

* * *

An hour of resting on the couch had helped him to recover from the hot and explosive sex they'd just had. He hadn't meant to be that rough with her, but when she touches him and needs him, he at times turns into an animal. She was now fast asleep in his arms, and he moved slowly to carry her to bed. He didn't want her to wake up alone and scared, so he carried her to his bed, exactly where he wanted her to be anyway.

He lowered her under the covers and slipped in beside her. She groaned as he pulled her naked body into his arms, but she quickly settled into his nook and slept. He had one leg in between her legs, as she continued to breathe him in… and he couldn't have been happier. But he actually was, but not for the reasons you'd think.

Yes, he was happy she was in his bed, and living with him, even if it was on a temporary basis. *Yes*, he was happy he didn't get caught stalking her, and that she trusted him enough to actually talk to him about the stalker. But he was most happy knowing that he'd successfully distracted her enough so she didn't remember to take that second pink pill. Not to mention the fact that he'd just had mind-blowing sex with her for the *second* time…without a condom.

Chapter 18

I was not alone. Someone was here. I ran out of my bedroom and into a man, a man who immediately grabbed me. I kicked and screamed, but I was no match for his brute strength as he aggressively clutched my arms, and pulled my body to his. "NO! Get out! NO! Don't touch me!" I yelled, as I frantically tried to free myself, from the man who grabbed me. The one who I'd noticed was wearing all black. The one who appeared to have on a dark colored cap that had *NY* embedded on it.

The one who was inside my small apartment right now, in the middle of the night. The one who's been *stalking* me. Panic was already taking over my mind, and I didn't know what to do. I didn't have time to call the police. I didn't have time to call anyone. He was here, right now… glaring at me in anger or was that need? *How did he get in again? Why was this happening to me?* He stood there motionless for a very long minute, just staring at me, from behind his dark shades.

Until I broke free and began to run from him, glancing behind me only once. But he wasted no time, and lunged after me, growling. I didn't know what he wanted from me and by the look on his face, I didn't want to find out. His strong arms quickly captured me, and as our bodies collided his dark shades had fell off his face.

Before I could get a look at his face, he turned me away from him, and pressed me into the wall. I was now facing the wall in front of me, panting in fear, as he then pushed himself closer to me. His hard body covering my soft body like a winter coat, totally sheltering me in. I could feel his muscular chest hard against my semi naked back, and his legs on my either side of my hips. My white camisole and grey leggings, did nothing to shield this man's frame from my body.

So I could feel whatever it was that he wanted me to feel, as his body sheltered mine, in width and strength. He continued to hold me close, so close that his breath came onto my neck in harsh winds, making the hairs on my neck stand up in fear. As I shuffled around and against him, he growled and tightened his hands around both my arms, keeping me exactly where he wanted me.

On impulse I stomped on his boot, hoping the pain would allow me to escape him, but it didn't. I screamed and cried out for help, but it seemed that no one could hear my cries, since no one came to help me. I expected him to yell at me, or to threaten me for my cooperation. But he said nothing, nothing at all. I could only hear his breathing, the harsh breathing of the man who watched me. I closed my eyes, as my fear consumed my entire being. There I was; alone, isolated, and scared. *What did he want?*

He was so close to me... so close on my body as I found myself taking deep breaths of him in. In that moment I could smell something... something familiar had pinged my nostrils. How could I recognize anything about this stranger, outside of his attire and shadow? The thought made me immediately stop yelling for help, and I froze while in his arms. *What was that scent?*

He suddenly began to shake my body vehemently, and I began to twist and turn, trying to get away from him again. But his arms tightened, trying to subdue me and my screams got louder. He released one of my arms and I turned my head and bit his arm hard, before he groaned.

"Jessica, stop this. Wake up!" *How does he know my name?* I then felt cold water being sprinkled on my face. *What? Where is that water coming from? Is he crying? Where are his tears?* "Baby, wake up," he yelled.

My eyes fluttered open to see a man leaning over me, looking at me intensely. I blinked a few times, vision somewhat blurry, as I looked at this man. I gasped, trying to breathe, as he cupped one side of my face. He just stared into my eyes with an intensity that looked vaguely familiar, but I could hardly see straight. I think I was still dreaming or was I?

I stretched my arms and realized that I was in bed with Thomas, and was just having a bad dream. But by the look on his face, I obviously had woke him up. "Are you alright?" He grumbled, and I immediately recognize *that* voice. It had warmth to it, with a slight rasp. It was the same voice of the one who saved me that night… the voice of my, **stalker**.

Oh My God!

I couldn't blink. I could barely breathe, and I was completely frozen as my mind started racing. *No, it couldn't be him.* Professor Brennan couldn't be the man who had been stalking me. No, there is no way! *Why would he do something like that?* He wouldn't scare me half to death, and then want me to live with him in his… I looked back at him as I began gasping for air. He then jumped off the bed, and grabbing the phone.

I continued to gasp for air as my thoughts roamed over my relationship with Thomas. We saw one another all the time during my time in his classes, for years. We were always appropriate with each other ever since I'd met him, but now all that has definitely changed. *Now we were lovers.*

"Yes, Dr. Klein, it's an emergency. My girlfriend was having a bad dream, and I think she is in a state of shock," he yelled. *Girlfriend?* "She's not talking or moving, and I had to sprinkle water on her face to even wake her up. Yes, she is breathing, but it's more like she's gasping for air," he frantically yelled into his phone. There was a long pause, as the doctor spoke to him.

"I don't know, should I call nine-one-one?" He yelled.

"No… Thomas, I'm fine," I muttered, my voice was small, as I moved to sit upward. His head snapped around and he ran over to me, before cupping my head with his hands, and looking deep into my eyes. My head was pounding and my heart was breaking, and I didn't truly understand why.

"Baby, are you okay? Dr. Klein can be here soon?" He urged.

"No, I umm, just had a bad dream… it happens," I gave him a tight smile, hoping that it would reassure him.

"Okay, baby…. if you say so. Are you sure?" He obviously doubted what I'd said.

"Yes, I am. Excuse me," I hurried off his

bed and instead of heading to his in-suite bathroom, I headed out his door. Once out of his room, I glanced back and saw him staring at me with a perplexed face. I hurried down the hall towards the guest bedroom, and quickly headed into the in-suite bathroom. Once inside, I closed the door and ran the faucet water. I then sat on the toilet, and exhaled the breath I was holding.

For some odd reason, I felt as if I could finally breathe. I sat in silence as the faucet water ran, and I thought back to last night. Where we had dinner and watched a movie just like any couple would do, after a few glasses of wine. We then made love, Thomas and I fuck like a couple that had been together for years. He handles my body as if he'd studied every crevice of it, during the few times we'd been intimate.

Professor Brennan was the only man to really show any real interest in me, romantically or otherwise. He'd always recommend that I take his extra-credit seminars, or stay after class for group studying, and I would always happily agree. When he touched me, I have never felt so wanted in my entire life. He more than wanted me. He craved me in ways I didn't think were even possible. Did he always crave this level of intimacy with me? Was all of this a part of his master plan? Am I his *obsession?*

"Oh. My. God," I choked out, as the vomit inched higher up my throat. The clues had always been there, but now I could see them clearly. He would be the only one that would *want* me enough to do this. I knew that he would go to any lengths to have me. But would that really include watching me?

His frame matched the one I'd seen months ago of the stalker. His voice didn't carry the rasp his did, but most voices only had that at given times. His eyes were the same of the man who saved me, and his touch was of one starving for the affection of only one woman. ME!! He had told me he'd wanted more with me, and he wanted to be with me in ways I hadn't even considered yet. He welcomed me into his home and was willing to give or be anything I needed.

He was so sweet and caring, and was an *amazing* lover. He made me feel like no other woman could do anything for him, and that I was his only craving. I knew that I secretly craved his touch and his kiss, but how was I supposed to feel when he lied and secretly watched me like some lunatic? He listened so attentively to me tell him all about the stalker yesterday, and he seemed so confident in saying that it would stop now, since the police were involved.

Which was something that I didn't think of, but now I knew why he said that. It wasn't because the sirens and police presence might have scared *him* away. It was because he now had what he wanted... I was right here with him.

Right here in his home, making love to him, eating and connecting with him and falling for him even more with every moment that I'm with him. He watched me, manipulated me, and now he scared the hell out of me. I felt the vomit in my throat again, trying to come up. *Knock. Knock.* "Jess, baby?" He called from outside the bathroom door. I leapt off the toilet, falling to my knees, as the vomit began to come up.

I retched in the toilet repeatedly, at the severity of this situation and the insanity of his pursuits. The door flew open and he stormed inside, dropping to his knees and rubbing my back, comforting me. I wanted to shove him off of me. I wanted to yell that I knew it was him, but I was so exhausted and racked with dry heaves that I allowed him to comfort me. But I loved his touch, his warmth, his sincerity, and his need for me. OMG! I was insane.

I can't love my stalker!!! I doubled over once more, as the vomit came up again, and I heard him on the phone with Dr. Klein telling him to come over. I went to protest, but another wave of vomit came out of my mouth, splattering onto the floor and all over the toilet seat.

"Jesus, Jess, let me help you, baby," he murmured, laying a towel over the splattered vomit, and pulling me up slightly to wipe my mouth. I looked at him, dazed and confused, as he ran the cloth under the cold water and dabbed my face. "Dr. Klein is on the way, baby. You'll be fine. I promise."

"Crackers, ginger ale?" I uttered, he nodded and kissed my head.

"Be right back, keep this cloth on your head," he ordered, before running out of the bathroom and down the stairs like a madman. I lay on the toilet seat feeling as if my world was crumbling, and there was nowhere to run. I had conflicted emotions on what I should do, and what I wanted to do. I had so many questions, but I was scared of the answers.

I pulled myself off the floor, feeling as if the vomiting was over, and I moved my body towards the sink. I splashed water on my face and reached for my toothbrush, when Thomas came back in the bathroom with crackers and two mini bottles of ginger ale.

"Baby, I'm sorry I took so long, your clothes delivery is here."

They're bringing them up right now, but I have your crackers and ginger ale. The doctor should be here any moment..." he rambled nervously, and I couldn't understand why my sickness made him so nervous. I was the one sick for goodness sake. He lifted a cracker to my mouth and I shook my head, as I silently watched him in the mirror.

I brushed my teeth and rinsed with mouthwash and let him help me to the bed. Where I then took a few sips of the ginger ale, as I climbed in the bed in the guest-room. He then went to re-wet the cloth for my head, and was folding it as he laid it on my head. He sat my warm soda and small plate of crackers on the night stand, as he held my hand. I felt so much better after I ate a few of the crackers, he'd fed me.

All this time I was thinking that this was the beginning of a new and fresh relationship, in the beginning phases of blooming. But to my horror, all this may have *not* been random at all. It all may have been structured, by my very own professor. The one who was feeding me another cracker as we speak, while gazing at me intensely, as if he was feeling *all* the pain and anguish I was feeling.

"Better?" He asked, and I nodded as I gazed back at him. I couldn't speak, there were no words to say out of my mouth. I just continued to look at him, in his eyes... the eyes of my **stalker.**

Chapter 19

The personal shoppers brought bag after bag of items inside the guest room for me. There was a small team of four, for the mass delivery. There were boxes of shoes, heels, and boots, and bags of undergarments, including lingerie. There were pant suits, skirts, dresses, jeans, accessories, and sweaters. This man ordered me an *entire* wardrobe.

He directed them to arrange all the items in the walk in closet, and on top of and inside the chest dresser drawers. As I just continued to lay there, silently, as he occasionally came over and dabbed my head with the cool cloth, and feed me a cracker. When he wasn't near me, I felt his eyes on me, and when I looked over at him, he would wink at me.

After the unpacking was finished and he had signed on the dotted line, he then walked them out. I sat back and exhaled, and closed my eyes. I felt like I was in the twilight zone, again. I didn't know how I should be feeling right now.

Should I be happy or angry? Should I be

scared or calm? Should I just leave or confront him? I was literally torn in two. He then walked back in the room, and he wasn't alone. There was an older gentlemen with him, who I assumed to be the doctor. He was dressed in a suit, with warm brown eyes and grey hair. His eyes were full of wisdom and I could tell almost immediately that he was very knowledgeable, about life.

"Jessica, this is Dr. Klein," Thomas introduced him, as he made his way over to me. I sat up a little and gave him a tight smile.

"Hello, it's nice to meet you, Dr. Klein," I muttered, clearing my throat.

"You too, Jessica. So I hear you're not feeling well today?" His voice was one of concern, so much concern it seemed odd at first. But he was a doctor, so he was concerned for the wellbeing of all people, I suppose.

"Yeah, I guess not," I uttered.

"Baby, Dr. Klein has always been my family's personal physician, as well as a personal friend. I trust him completely," he stated proudly.

"Thanks for the compliment, Thomas, but

let's get her checked out. May I?" He turned to me and I nodded. Dr. Klein then moved towards me, with his doctor bag full of goodies.

"Um, Thomas?" I called.

"Yes, baby?" He was at my side in a second, and I handed him the empty plate from on the side table. "More?" He asked, as he smiled.

"Please," I smiled back at him. He took the plate from me and leaned down and kissed my head.

"As you wish. Can you eat anything? You still haven't had breakfast yet," he asked.

"Maybe a toasted English muffin, and a few pieces of bacon would be fine," I suggested.

"Okay, baby, no problem. Dr. Klein will take care of you," he stated, and then turned to the doctor. "Anything for you, Peter?"

"No, thank you, Thomas," Dr. Klein replied. He then headed out the door and I exhaled, and relaxed into my pillow.

"He makes you nervous?" He smiled, as he checked my pulse. *If he only he knew!*

"I guess he does, but only sometimes," I replied.

"Yes, he can be very intense, but he is a

good boy, considering..." he muttered, and checked my temperature.

"Considering what?" I asked, before he placed the thermometer in my mouth.

"Did you know his family?" He asked.

"No, I haven't met them yet," I mumbled. Wait, he said...*did*...didn't he? *As in past tense? As in no longer here?*

"Ah, so you don't know what happened to them," he stated, and I saw emotion covering his face.

"What happened?" I asked, as he checked my temperature.

"I'm not sure I should be the one to talk to you about this—"

"Please, he hasn't told me yet," I pleaded, hoping that he could give me some insight to this complicated, crazy man.

"Well, Thomas family was killed on a plane, fifteen years ago," he stated, and I gasped and swallowed loudly, as he looked up at me. "They didn't take Thomas with them on the trip, because he begged them to stay and attend some meet and greet with his cousin. Professors Abigale Brennan and Thomas Brennan Sr, were very accomplished and respected," he sighed.

"They are truly missed by their friends, family, and students at Berkeley. They were returning from a tour of a volcano in Hawaii, both his parents and younger sister, Maggie, was on the plane."

"That is horrible! How has he dealt with all this?" I was flabbergasted, this was such a tragedy and my heart cried for him. To be so young and to lose his family, must had devastated him.

"He was in therapy for a while, and he lived with an aunt and uncle, until he went to college. Then he decided to become a professor, to honor them. I think his goal in that alone, really helped him to overcome the shock of losing his family."

"That couldn't have been an easy goal, living up to your parent's legacy, at their school nonetheless."

"It wasn't. He would call me sometimes to talk, and I would give him what he needed to hear, so that he wouldn't quit. So that he would see his goal through, and he did," he smiled as his words flowed from his mouth, like a proud father would. I smiled, and I immediately liked him even more.

"Thank you for telling me this, truly."

"He is intense, but he has a great heart. He was always closed off to the opposite sex, afraid of being attached to anyone, for some reason. But not now, not with you. The fear and panic I saw and heard, once he opened the door for me, was something I hadn't seen from him in years."

"Really? I hardly know who he is or what he wants, or needs."

"He needs you to be okay, Jessica. You mean something to him, and I can tell that he means something to you as well. So, do you have any idea why you are sick?" He asked.

"Huh, oh umm…I haven't done anything out of the normal, if that's what you're asking," I muttered, dazed at his previous statements.

"Have you taken any drugs, prescription or otherwise?"

"No, I haven't taken any—" I froze mid-statement as realization dawned on me.

"Hey, what is it…what have you taken?" He asked urgently, registering the horror on my face.

"It's not what I've taken. It's what I haven't taken," I sucked in a deep breath as I closed my eyes, chastising myself.

"I don't follow, Jessica?"

"I had taken a morning after pill, night before last. I was supposed to take the other one yesterday," I muttered.

"And did you?"

"I forgot," I uttered. *Oh my GOD!*

"Oh my. I don't need to tell you that without that second dose, at the exact time recommended, the intended results will be ineffective," he replied, in the exact way I read that disclaimer off the damn box yesterday.

"No, you don't need to tell me that," I snapped.

"I will write you a prescription for birth control, but you need to rest today and tomorrow. Do you need a letter for work?" He asked, totally ignoring my irritation at my forgetfulness.

"No, I am supposed to start a new job tomorrow," I murmured.

"Jessica, you have to take care of you first. You're weak, and nauseous I presume, so you will need to rest. I will give you documentation for your employer, and a prescription for birth control, and one for motion sickness. But I would recommend that you see your doctor in a few weeks, to see if you're pregnant or not. Depending on your cycle and ovulation…it may be too late to rule out the fact that you're not," he stated, as I signed.

"Oh God," I uttered.

"Baby, I made you some coffee, too, in case you wanted some," Thomas announced, as he re-entered the room, and both Dr. Klein's and my head popped up.

"Well, I'll be on my way then," Dr. Klein announced. I watched as Thomas's smile dropped, and his face was immediately filled with anxiety. "She will be fine, Thomas. She needs rest, food, and no alcohol or wine for the next few days," he murmured to him, then turned to me and smiled. "Let me write your prescriptions and I'll email you a letter for your work, Jessica," he then pulled out his pad and began to scribble on it.

Thomas walked over and laid a cloth napkin over my lap, and set my plate over it, while placing my coffee on the side table. He'd made bacon, sausage and toasted two English muffins, one with butter and one with jelly. *He was just too much sometimes.* I looked up at him and found myself grinning at how attentive he was to me. When he noticed that I was smiling at him, the slow grin that took over his anxiety-ridden face, was simply breathtaking.

"Thank you," I replied, as he gazed at me.

"Anything for you, baby, I lo—"

"Here you go, Jessica. You're all set. Now remember my recommendations for later," he walked over and shook my hand and then shook Thomas's, before leaving my prescriptions on the table, next to my cup of coffee.

"It was very nice meeting you, Jessica. Take care of yourself," he stated, but I wasn't paying attention. I was still staring at Thomas, who was in turn, staring nervously back at me.

"Thank you, Dr. Klein," he uttered warily, never taking his eyes off of me. He was about to say the L word. I knew it, and I felt it. His face, his eyes, and his shaky breaths confirmed it. *HOLY COW!!!*

"Thomas, I'll see myself out, and please call

me if you need me," Dr. Klein stated, and then he left the room. Thomas was seated on the side of my bed next to me, his hand on my arm, and his eyes nervously on mine. *He loved me? Did he really? How could he love me so soon?* I was deep in thought, while my eyes stayed locked on his.

I knew what I wanted to ask him, but I couldn't find the words. I didn't have to worry about that for too much longer, because he actually beat me to the punch.

Chapter 20

"So, are you ready to tell me what your dream was about?" He calmly asked.

"You," I said flatly.

"Me? You were dreaming about me, and you panicked like that?" He looked at me, as if I had actually insulted him with my answer. "What was I doing in this dream?" he uttered, gauging my reaction.

"I think you know *exactly* what you were doing in my dream already?" I snarled, and he flinched back from my anger. I was trying to stay calm, but I was quickly becoming overwhelmed again. All the info Dr. Klein had told me about his family, his stalker capabilities, a possible pregnancy, and his…love for me had me spent

"What are you talking about?" He asked.

"Thomas, I know," I said, looking him square in the face.

"Know what?" He feigned innocence, and it pissed me off even more.

"Don't play anymore games with me. No

more, do you understand me?" My voice became louder with every word. "I. Fucking. Know." My breathing had turned into harsh pants, as my anger began to rise. His ability to purposely not comprehend me, or admit to his actions would not be tolerated. He lied and manipulated me, and only was incompetent when it was convenient for him and his goals. Until now, because now… I wanted the truth and he was going to give that to me, whether he wanted to or not.

He just stared at me, his face a complete blank and devoid of any emotion, which made it impossible for me to read. "I only have one question, and before you lie, think hard about your answer, Professor. If I don't like your answer, or if it's *another* lie… *you* won't ever see *me* again," he gasped and closed his eyes, as if my words had literally cut him. As if the thought of not seeing me took away his breath, and he couldn't fathom the thought of not having me. Which was shocking and scary all in itself.

"Tell me…why?" I muttered, and braced myself for his answer.

He then opened his eyes as he exhaled, blinking nervously at me. I could see the mist covering his eyes, as he gazed silently at me. I knew he realized that his answer would confirm my assumptions of him, and also expose his motives for his actions. He was very silent, as he gazed at me and I at him. The only thing I could hear was our breathing. *Why couldn't he answer me? Why was he doing this?* The minutes steadily passed with nothing being said between us, but our eyes stayed locked, and I could see him thinking about how to respond. I really didn't know what started all of this, and what had made him begin to—

"Because I'm in love with you," he choked out, and I gasped. *Oh shit.*

"Thomas, ugh, how can you be so sure that you love a woman you've only slept with a few times?" I asked, perplexed, while still digesting his declaration of love. Sherry was right, he really did want a life with me. *Oh my god!*

"It's never been about the sex. I loved you before we ever made love, and I don't think I can help it," he looked sheepishly at me, and I swallowed rather loudly.

"Are you crazy, Thomas? Should I be scared of you?"

"I am *not* crazy, and I have *no* shame regarding my feelings for you, Jessica. I love you so much, and I couldn't wait to get closer to you, so I progressed in the only way that I could," he said.

"So you, stalked me?"

"I ensured that you were safe," he replied.

"By following me?"

"By making sure that you made it to and from your destinations," he countered.

"You can't say it, can you?" I demanded.

"I won't say it, because it's not true. I am not some delusional obsessed maniac of a man. I am a man who has found his future wife, and I want to be everything she needs, in every way," he explained, and then exhaled a long breath. As if he's been wanting to say that to me for years.

"How long have you been in love with me, Professor?" I whispered.

"A while," he muttered, and I could feel my emotions at bay. How could all of this happen to me without me knowing? I was not understanding how he was doing all this, and why?

"Do you think that's fair to me? You manipulated me. You drove me crazy. You-you…" I felt myself getting choked up again.

"I know, and I'm sorry. But you were still in school and I had to keep my distance, literally. But that's over now, and I know we can work it all out, together," he stated expectantly, as if I felt as strongly for him, as he did for me.

"How do you know if that's what I want to do, huh? I mean, I just figured out that you've been *stalking* me. That it was *you* who saved my life that night, when I was drunk. You!" I yelled.

"Jessica," he began to speak.

"No, you've been lying and manipulating me this whole time. I even feel like you've been with me longer than I've been with you, at this point. How is that even right? Then, you make love to me with no protection and now I may be pregnant," I exhaled harshly.

"Is that what Dr. Klein said?" He asked incredulously, which made me scoff at him.

"You can wipe that smile off of your face, Thomas. This is not a joke. I can't afford a child. I don't even have a *career* yet," I yelled, panicked, and feeling completely overwhelmed.

"Baby, please calm down. We will be fine, I have a trust fund that I haven't even touched yet. It's been accruing interest for over two decades now, so we're good. We will always be good, I promise you," he squeezed my hand, and I gasped. He then raised his hand and slowly ran his thumb over my bottom lip, tempting me to *bite* him.

"So, what then Professor? Oh let me guess…we run away together and buy some land in Florence, and we just live there together forever?" I asked sarcastically.

"I was thinking more of an island, but your idea of Italy works too. As long as you're mine completely, and in every way. I know I will be happy where ever we are," he quickly said.

"Completely and in every way, what does that mean?"

"It means…becoming my *wife,*" he stated firmly. *His what???* I found myself shaking my head and giggling, at this insane man.

"Sounds like the American dream; wife, mother, and married to a professor with a trust fund." I pursed my lips and he smiled. He then pressed his thumb onto my lips, and I kissed it gently.

"I could be a dream maker. Your dream maker, baby… only yours, Jessica Moore," he whispered, as his eyes lowered to the thumb he'd placed on my lips, and his eyes clouded with desire.

"So, it all wasn't random… you're courting me was all structured then?" I asked.

"Some parts yes, but some was random, too."

"Why do you trust me so much? Why do you want me?" I flinched my eyes, not fully understanding. The man had fan clubs, and possibly the best mouth on the planet, if you asked me. So why me? He smiled softly and his lips twitched, while he drifted off in deep thought.

"You're everything I've always wanted…in a student, a girlfriend, a wife, and a best friend. I realized that a very long time ago, Jessica. From the moment you grilled me in front of everyone, in your very first class. For that entire first year, I saw more in you that peaked my interest.

Things progresses of their own accord, the more time we spent together. My feelings had started to quickly evolve, and I needed more, but I took what I could get. I'm sorry, Jessica, for what I've put you through. I'm sorry for lying to be near you, but I'll never be sorry for loving you. Or for needing and craving you, and your touch. You're intoxicating scent even drives me crazy. You mean everything to me," he stated and then exhaled.

I just looked at him, and could clearly see his passion and desperation to have me. That alone was intoxicating in itself.

"So where are your *stalker* clothes?" I muttered, as he chuckled.

"In a duffle bag, in other guestroom's closet. I will throw them out today, I promise," he stated firmly.

"You know, I could have you arrested?" I twitched my lips playfully.

"I know," he smirked and I smiled.

"You're crazy," I sighed.

"Only for you," he said. Maybe he was only crazy for me, was that so bad? This man had lost his family and doesn't even date, and he has plenty of woman who would just love to get their slimy paws on him. But he doesn't give any of them his attention, because he is only focused on me. I just sit and stare at him, wondering why I'm not running away from him or calling the police. *He is my stalker!*

"I want to do something," I stated.

"Okay, what is it, baby?" He asked.

"Take this." I then handed him the plate and the napkin, and he'd sat it on the nightstand. I pulled back the covers and climbed out of the bed, while holding onto his arm. I stood in front of him, as he looked down at me in panic, waiting for me to either run or slug him. I moved closer to him and grabbed his belt buckle, pulling him closer to me.

I began to unfasten his belt and pants, as he gasped in shock. They fell to his ankles and I then ran my hand down his uncovered erection, as he hissed and growled in his throat. I lowered to my knees, and glanced back up at him, but he looked as if he was about to faint.

He had the face of someone who was looking at the winning jackpot ticket, his eyes wide, face frozen and mouth gaping open. I realized that I hadn't really tasted him yet, and before I made any decision about our future relationship, I wanted and needed to have that experience under my belt. I had never sucked his cock, and I could only imagine how many times he'd fantasized about me doing just that. I could see it written all over his face. All over his uneasy face.

"Baby?" He uttered, desire thick in his tone.

"Hmmm," I sung, as I slowly ran my tongue up the length of his cock, and his breath began coming in harsh pants. I slowly licked up his twitching cock a few more times, until I knew that he desperately needed me to insert him into my mouth.

I wanted to drive him crazy with need, desire and lust. I needed to. I'd never really considered myself a professional at giving a blowjob, but with Thomas, I knew it didn't matter. Everything I did, whether good or bad, was always more than enough for him.

Crap, he really does love me.

He tasted salty and sweet, an addictive combination for me to endure if I stayed with him. I could hear him growling above me, and I smiled inside, because I was now uncaging the beast in him. I could tell that he was truly in distress, and from the guttural noises escaping him, he was already at the point of no return and it'd only been sixty seconds. I needed to see this beast, and how much control he had over himself, once this beast was unleashed.

I twirled my tongue around his cock, sliding it over and around my lips, but never inserting him. I was driving him mad, as he went from trembling, to his stance now hardening beneath my fingers. "*Fuck, baby, please,*" he growled.

"I want you to take my mouth, Professor. Grab my hair and feed me your cock, in the exact way you want me to have it. Use my mouth, Professor, now." His hands were buried in my hair in that next second, as he guided my face towards the tip of his cock. I then took him inside my mouth in one hard and swift motion, closing my lips around him with all the strength I could muster up. He roared like a bear, tilting his head back as he trembled, while hardening inside my mouth.

I took him deeper, until he was filling my mouth with his small thrusts, near the very back of my throat. I slowly pulled him all the way back out and then right back in, deep inside. He groaned loudly while his hands tightened in my hair, silently telling me that he wanted more. I began a rhythm, a rhythm of driving him mad, just as he did to me last night. But he tasted so good, and I found myself losing my battle to keep control of this situation.

I was beginning to enjoy this too much, as I began to moan around his cock. I teased him with my lips and tongue, plopping him out of my mouth occasionally, as he exhaled a harsh breath.

I began to tease the very tip of him, before I licked up his balls to the very tip of his cock, and ensnared him back into my mouth while sucking faster and harder. "Fuckkkk!" He growled, and moved against my mouth, panting and groaning loudly. "Take me, baby. Take it…it's all yours," He growled again, as he prepared to release.

I grasped his shaft up near the tip, right under the ridge. I began to pump him and flick my tongue around the head, in rotating flicks, licks and sucks while he roared like a bear.

Once I knew he was on the very brink, as pre-cum began spurting from him. I then took him fully into my mouth, and he came... *hard*.

I sucked and lapped at him, until he stumbled two steps away from me, while making the most erotic sounds I'd ever heard in my entire life. He was barely breathing and as he opened his eyes to look at me. I stood, while lifting his pants back up to his waist as he grabbed them. He was speechless. He was beyond satisfied. The man was floating. His eyes were twinkling, and his face had a grin that nothing could wipe away. But as it turns out, I had the words to do the job, and my words did manage to wipe his grin completely away.

"Thomas?" I muttered, licking my lips, as his eyes lowered to them.

"Hmm, baby?" He asked.

"Get out of here, and don't come back, not until I call you from my phone and tell you to come back here." His face had transformed in a matter of a millisecond; grin gone, smile forgotten, as devastation covered him. "I'm sorry, but I need some time to myself. I have my laptop, so I will email my job about everything soon. I just want to think. I need to, and either I can do that here, or at a hotel?" I stated.

"O…K, are you sure you don't—" he began to offer.

"I'm sure, I just need some time. Can you give me that, please?" I pleaded.

"Anything you need, baby," he breathed.

"Okay, good," I exhaled, and started to feel calm already.

"Can I have a kiss?" He asked me. He looked so sexy from his orgasmic high, that I couldn't deny him that kiss.

"Sure, you can have—" His lips were on mine in a flash. His hands in my hair, his body pressed against mine, and we fell back onto the bed. He had literally attacked me, as he rubbed himself against my slickness, and I moaned into his mouth.

He must have known that I was aroused from sucking his cock, and my God was he right. His hand entered my pants quickly, delving inside of my underwear as we kissed. I found myself bucking my hips against him as he touched me, needing to feel him. As he slid his fingers around my slickness, teasing me, I gasped.

"Oh God…" I whimpered against his mouth.

"I know, baby, I know," he muttered, and kissed me again, as his fingers roamed around my slickness once, then twice more, before he plunged two fingers deep inside me.

"Oh yes, oh fuck," I cried, I was in an instant coma of sensations. In a matter of seconds he had consumed me whole. His mouth consumed me, his fingers consumed me, and his body consumed me as well. I could feel him everywhere, my body was his to take and devour. He frantically tugged off my pants, as I tried to stop him. "No, we shouldn't, Thomas," I told him.

"We should, baby, tell me I can have you…tell me I can?" He sat back on his knees, rubbing his hand up and down his newly erect cock. The man was staring at me as if he wanted to eat me alive. He was growling with need with each second that passed.

I knew that I wanted him, and my body needed him, as I trembled with desire of my own. I could feel his need for me, his desire was so deep and raw. I knew that I needed him, and I still wanted him, too, in my own way. We both really did need each other and in that moment, I knew that that *need* wouldn't just go away. Our connection, the infatuation, the love and the need to be near him, it all meant something. *I loved him.*

"Take me, take me, Thomas," I responded with so much raw hunger that his eyes widened, and he smiled at me wickedly, as I smiled back at him. Once he saw that I had no doubts in what I had said to him, he lunged towards me. He kissed me deeply, moving that talented mouth of his all over my body with an unquenchable hunger. Once he'd reached my cunt, he began kissing all over my inner thighs, while lifting my leg up in the air as he devoured me whole.

It wasn't long at all before I'd started pulsating and contracting around his tongue, as he groaned into me. He continued to devour me in that way, sopping me up with his mouth and tongue, and using his fingers to sweeten his gestures even more.

After the third orgasm he'd given me with his mouth, he then slammed his cock inside me, as we both screamed out in ecstasy. My back arched and my head was titled towards the ceiling, as I dug my nails into his back, hearing him groan in delight at the mild pain. He moved his hands under me, digging his fingers into my ass as he moved on top of me, pulling me into him even deeper.

Screaming and moaning, biting and sucking, groping and savagely kissing, was us for the next seven or eight minutes. Or better yet…the next seven or eight months. We became completely submerged in a place that felt so right, so perfect, and so us. A place where we dwelled openly together in the light of day, as well secretly in the night. A place where we *both* were hopelessly in love and completely lost… in each other.

Epilogue

A year later...

Professor Brennan

I laid in our bed thinking back to the day of our wedding, the day she became my wife. It was a gorgeous and sunny day, and all kinds of emotions were running through me. None being anything other than excitement, pure joy and determination. I was marrying the woman who had captured my heart that day. A woman named Jessica. I wasn't nervous about saying I do, I was only a bit nervous about reciting my wedding vows to her, without becoming too emotional. I mean who would actually want to see a grown man crying? *Not me!*

I had no doubts whatsoever that I was making the right decision, by marrying the love of my life today. She was who I wanted, and this was a day I had dreamed about for a while now. It was finally happening. I stood near the front of the church in my black tux, with a friend by my side. A good friend of mine named Mark, who I'd met in college. He was always a bachelor, even back then.

So the idea of settling down and getting married wasn't exactly in his immediate future. But we were close, Mark and myself, as opposites attract in relationships, they also attract in friendships as well. Mark was a man who truly enjoyed the single life, and had no plans to change that. I only hoped that one day he could find a woman to complete him, just like Jessica does for me. But you know what they say... *old habits die hard.*

There weren't many in attendance for our small impromptu wedding, just a few friends and family members from each side. I wanted our wedding to be exactly how she wanted it to be and she wanted a very small wedding in a church, and that's what we had. When I heard the wedding march being played, I knew the time was winding down, and soon after, I was a married man.

The fact that I still reminisce about our wedding day almost daily, was just insane. But to awaken with the one you loved so desperately, holding you, or touching you, was absolutely wonderful. I absolutely loved the view of seeing my wife first thing in the morning. Just seeing her lying there, or holding her in my arms...was more than I could ever wish for. I was a goner and now, she was all mine.

There she was, right where she belonged, right here with me. I found myself admiring her, as my hand gently slid across her swollen belly with awe and appreciation. The belly that now sheltered my unborn son inside. Jessica was amazing in every way, and seeing her pregnant enhanced my need for her tenfold.

I loved seeing her hair fanned over her pillow, while her intoxicating scent covered our bed. I could hear her small deep breaths gently escaping her lungs, ensuring me that she and my son were getting enough oxygen. I would be lying if I said I didn't worry about her even more, now that she was carrying our child. This was a critical time, a time when my entire family was inside of one body. Her body. I knew how lucky I was to have her, and I still found our journey thus far to be uniquely amazing. I loved it.

My lips inadvertently found her back and I puckered my lips, planting soft kisses across her shoulder blade and up the nape of her neck. She slept so deeply nowadays, being pregnant made her very tired and restless. But I knew it wouldn't be long before she was awake and moaning my name. My wife would always wake up to my touch, and that was not up for negotiation.

I couldn't keep my hands off her, nonetheless, so that would never be an issue for me. She was my morning and my night, and everything in between. Her smile made my heart jump, her body drove me mad with desire. Her skin was smooth and soft, and glowed fluorescently, hypnotizing my eyes with a lust so strong that I still couldn't control it. The taste of her gave me a special kind of high, a high that I secretly craved every day now. Having full access to her sweetness, was just bliss. I could barely go a few hours without it.

Which is why my face was *now* buried in between her legs, tasting her sweetness yet again. I glanced up at her, to see her gripping our sheets, arching her back into me as she moaned. I needed to awaken her in this way. I needed the first sounds I heard in the morning to be the sounds of her pleasure. I needed the first taste of my day to be *her*, not toothpaste, mouthwash or coffee…just her.

I needed her to come around my fingers, my tongue, or my cock before she left our bed each day. Our days needed to start and end with each other, and it did, with no exceptions. I actually wanted to feel connected to her in every way, every single day of my life.

Would I call myself obsessed?

I don't believe I am. I am just a man who is deeply in love with a woman named Jessica Brennan. The only woman I've actually wanted to share my life with. The only woman I loved long before I'd touched her, or even kissed her. The only woman I watched, and as she called it, "stalked" for her passion, warmth and her love.

She was the one I would always want, the one who I would be with forever. "Oh, Thomas…oh God," she moaned, as she shuddered beneath me, and I knew she was close. It was safe to say that I knew her body very well at this point. Her body and I had a very close, and intimate relationship. As she began panting, she came with a long groan, before I began sucking on her, making her body jerk into my mouth. Then she screamed as if she was in pain or in labor, but I knew different. Her climax was escalating right before my eyes, pulling her into a web of pleasure as she trembled in my arms.

She fell back on the pillows as I kissed up her thighs, over her belly, to her tender and swollen breasts, as she whimpered while writhing under me.

I knew what she needed, because it was the same thing I needed. I lay on my side, close to her backside, lifting her leg over mine, and slipped into her hard and strong. We both moaned loudly, as I grasped her waist. She was wet, hot and greedy for my cock now. I could tell that she was almost ready to come again, and that turned me on even more.

I loved that she wanted me so badly, and I knew that because *the body never lies*. I slowly flipped her over so she was on her hands and knees, and as I moved behind her. She was moaning already, just at the feel of me still inside her. I could feel her moistened walls sucking me into her even more, and I found myself growling as I got into position. I grabbed a handful of her hair, and she arched her back and moaned loudly. The sounds of her pleasure saturated my ears, and I loved every waking moment of it.

"Baby, this what you want?" I growled at her, feeling myself losing control, very fast. Jessica brought out this beast in me at times, and I became a man who was possessed with nothing, but pure lust and desire, *for her*. She actually loved the beast in me, not only from the pleasure, but also because she knew she was the only one who could sate him.

"Thomas, oh yes, please," she panted, as I pulled gently on the hair in my hand, tilting her head upward as I began to pull out of her. I could feel her walls contracting mildly with my withdrawal, while she trembled in my wake. I withdrew from her, and she mewled her disapproval. I smirked even though she couldn't see me. As my other hand gently played with her breast, kneading and pulling her swollen nipples, she groaned loudly.

"I want you, baby, only you," I whispered close to her ear and she trembled, as she rubbed her ass over my cock, tempting me to hurry and get back into her.

"I want you, inside of me—*now*," she whimpered, and I growled as I turned her head slightly, then traced the edge of her ear with my tongue.

"Is that an order, Mrs. Brennan?" I yanked her hair back slightly, as I bit down on her ear, causing her to cry out.

"NO! I-I'm sorry, professor, please forgive me," she pleaded, and I smiled and leaned up, releasing her hair. I slide my hand slowly down her back, feeling her hot and moistened skin beneath my fingers.

"Hmm, baby, you know I love it when you challenge me," I groaned, as I slid my cock up and down her entrance, teasing her and testing her. She was what they called a *pregnant sex fiend*. She wanted it all the time now, and I was only too happy to give it to her. But sometimes I wanted her to work for it, and play the game I wanted to play. Lucky for me, she was always happy to oblige, and I loved her even more for that.

I then pinched her hardened nipple and slammed into her at the same time, shocking her and her body into an immediate climax. She screamed my name, as her body tightened and released around my cock exquisitely. I found myself moaning and growling with each thrust of my hips into her plush ecstasy. As the intensity of her climax began to let up, I could tell that she was catching her second wind.

So I slowed my pace to give her a few moments to catch her breath, because her orgasms were so intense now that she was pregnant. Once she was ready, she then began to move back onto me, pushing me deeper into her. *A challenge?*

She wanted more, and she was never afraid to ask me, whether with her mouth or her body. I grasped her hips tighter and began to really lose myself in her, as I took her how she wanted and needed to be taken. She cried out as I groaned. I moaned as she moaned, I gasped when she gasped. We were in sexual sync, and it showed, as we both trembled. We were beyond sexually compatible. We were obsessed with each other, and deeply in love.

She is my wife, and she just loved to provoke me at times. She also liked to push and challenge me in ways I've never been challenged before. As we came apart together, I realized something in that moment, while my hot seed was being sucked out of me by her body. I realized that Jessica was just perfect for me. She was beautiful, she was bold, and she was all mine. How in the hell I got to be so lucky?

***

Jessica

I had no doubt a year ago that my destiny included Thomas in a more direct way than him just being my professor. I couldn't really call it fate, because he'd constructed most of our time together in his ploy to have me.

But I couldn't complain. To be wanted so intensely by a man as complex as Thomas was an honor, and also a bit frightening. But he and I were both very happy, and that's what really mattered. We were moving so fast in our relationship, that it sometimes scared me, as well as my family, and for good reason. But I didn't let it consume me, and I hoped they wouldn't either. I loved and respected my parents, but the truth was that I didn't need permission from them, or anyone else, to decide to get married or to move to Florence for a year.

Thomas liked to call it *our yearlong honeymoon,* but now we were soon heading back to the states. For the birth of our son, and I knew it would be a bittersweet trip. We hadn't even gotten there yet, and I was already anxious to go back to Florence. Where we could be alone and just be. After I agreed to be with him, completely. I told him that it would be on one condition, and before I even told him what that condition was, he agreed. *Crazy man.* But that was my dilemma in all this. I loved Thomas, and he was the man of my dreams, but was he *crazy?*

I needed him to understand the error of his ways, even though he had his own love-struck reasons of stalking me. It still didn't make it right, so I made him a deal. He had to re-enter therapy and talk to someone about his actions, and his future with me. So he had his private therapy sessions and we went to couple's therapy, for the next eight months. Being with him became a full time job, but at the end of those eight months. I knew for sure that he was the man for me, the one I'd be with for the rest of life, and I happily accepted his proposal for marriage.

He is wonderful man, and I found myself looking forward to those intoxicating looks he gave me, every time he saw me. Those sensual heated looks made me feel as if I was the luckiest girl in the world. The feeling of his warmth covering me, each and every day, not only calmed me, it excited me to. We'd been making love all morning today, and neither of us was ready to throw in the towel yet, even though it was almost noon. I didn't know about other households, but mornings in our house were always, and I do mean *always,* amazing.

This man had a ravenous hunger for me that just was unheard of, and I knew how extremely lucky I was to call him *my husband.*

"Oh, Baby..." he groaned, as I ran my hands

over his chest, feeling his soft prickly hairs under my fingertips, and admiring the toned and muscular cut of his chest and abs that were now glistening in our mingled sweat.

The heat from his skin warmed and soothed my semi-swollen fingers. The scent of our combined perspiration and arousal deeply fragranced our master bedroom. I needed him and his touch, and I wanted it all the time. Even more now, being pregnant. I touched his skin with my hands and my tongue, as he lay on his back. I just needed to taste him again. As I ran my tongue over his nipple, sucking it gently into my mouth, I could feel him tremble slightly beneath me, while growling.

I slowly circled my tongue around one nipple, and then the other one. I found myself nipping him harder, and sucking more intensely, as I closed my eyes, getting completely lost in the taste of him.

He was who I desired. His taste was what I craved, and his pleasure was what I needed to feel sated and satisfied. His fingertips alternated from massaging my scalp, to tightening in my hair, as I sucked and gently nipped his delicious cock.

"Oh, Fuck!" He growled. I had truly become as obsessed with him as he was with me.

I wasn't sure if it was my pregnancy hormones, or just my hormones in general, but who cared. He was my husband now, and the rest didn't matter to me. What I did know was that I not only wanted Professor Brennan, but I desperately needed him. I needed the taste of him on my lips, the smell of him saturating my nostrils. I needed to hear his pleasure in my ears, and feel him trembling from my touch. Our love was intense and insane, but it was ours.

I could feel his cock swelling in my mouth, and he pulled my head up gently, as he came gloriously on my breasts. I was seven months pregnant, and neither one of us felt comfortable with me *swallowing* at this point. So we agreed to venture from that extra-curricular activity, for the remainder of my pregnancy. Afterwards, we showered together and headed downstairs to the kitchen, with our arms around each other.

We loved holding one another, and it couldn't be helped. It was past noon now, and we were starving for food, but we were both sated on each other. Which was always the case, in the Brennan household. As we made our way into the kitchen that I loved. It was a classic Italian kitchen, stocked with everything we could ever need. Life in Florence was peaceful, and our own, exclusively.

We were practically living in our own world, where only the three of us existed. Even though life for us was moving fast, it was also exciting. I always wondered how I was so lucky to have a love like this "stalk" his way into my life. Life was good, and with the impending delivery of our son…life for us was more than good. It was just perfect.

THE END

Author Note

THANK YOU SO much for reading. Your reviews are very much welcomed. Want more KC Royale? Then subscribe to my monthly newsletter, or check out my new website Visit my pages to connect with me and keep up with all things KC. Listed below are my Social Media outlets:

Facebook, Goodreads, Twitter, TSU
Or feel free to email me at:
Kmarwrites@gmail.com

My next book will be out in July, 2015. Do you want to know the title, and perhaps read the synopsis?? Then by all means, flip the page already. XOXOXO

The Scent of... MUSK

Synopsis:

Two guys. One woman. She is attracted to both, but in two totally different ways. With one guy there is this magnetic pull to him, an intense physical attraction she can't control. The physical connection with this guy is so strong, that just a look or a touch from him, and she's in a trance of lust. But with the other guy, she feels safe, maybe for the first time in her life, with any man. There is this indescribable warmth, and emotive appeal about him, that she has never felt before. The emotional connection with this one guy, renders her speechless.

Susan's life has always been complicated, ever since she lost the last member of her family, a few years ago. She's had a hard time dealing with her loss, and how alone she secretly felt in this huge world. Taking life one day at a time, in work and in finding love, was her new motto. But one day she meets a man named Charleston Grayson, who challenges her and manages to help her to feel again. She can't stop thinking about him, no matter how much she tries to fight it. Until she reluctantly agrees to be a wing-man for her best friend's blind date, where her friend's date brings a wingman of his very own.

Susan somehow finds herself emotionally drawn to this man, almost immediately. A man who is a complete stranger to her. A man that she's met by chance. A man named Simon Parker.

Pre-order now on Amazon

More Books by Author KC Royale

Taken Love

Synopsis:

Your first crush isn't normally the man who ends up dating your best friend, nor is he the man you end up wanting to marry. But my inexperience on how to handle such a strong reaction to one guy nearly cost me everything back then. They say you can't control when you first fall in love or who you fall in love with. So when I found myself in love for the first time at seventeen, it was a bit shocking. But not for the reasons you think but then again, maybe it was.

His name was Johnathan Pierce, the one who drove me insane and frustrated me to no end. How could I not fall for him? How could any girl refuse his green eyes, experienced touch and intoxicating words? He was no longer the seventeen year old boy who had taken me for the ride of my life, he was a man now. It's been six years since my heart was taken by Johnathan, a man who was now a CEO of a billion dollar empire. A man who has taken all that I had to give and hurt me in the worst way imaginable, causing me to give up everything and run away. The indescribable pain I felt has consumed me for six long years now, but the time has come for me to return back home.

Home, where it all started for a girl name Kathleen Toth-Chamberlin. Every story has a beginning… and an end.

Buy now on Amazon

About the Author

KC Royale started writing at the tender age of nine years old. Being the only girl in a house with four brothers, she used writing as a way to occupy her time. Her curiosity grew into her creating poems, and short stories in various genres, which then grew into a love of writing all types of stories. Having grown up in the Washington Metropolitan Area, she got a lot of her inspiration from life, love and nature. She currently lives in Maryland with her family, and her ever-present laptop. When she is not writing she enjoys watching movies, cooking, traveling, and listening to soft rock music. She is also an avid reader who enjoys a good romance, erotica, or thriller to pass the time.

Acknowledgements

I will keep this short and very sweet; I have the most amazing Dream Team that anyone could have and you ALL are very much appreciated. To my team of editors, proofreaders, betas and promoters... I *Thank You*, so much for your hours of support and feedback on my draft. I want to thank a few special people, whom I love dearly: Tracy A, Dawn H, Elizabeth E, Arissa M, Amber S, SallyAnn C, Angie F, Hope W. I want to send a very special shout-out to my wonderful friend, Amanda P. You ladies are ALL loved and appreciated! To all the readers out there, keep on reading and I will keep on writing. **–KC**

Made in the USA
Middletown, DE
04 August 2015